The Gospel of the Spirit

The Gospel of the Spirit

A STUDY IN THE FOURTH GOSPEL

by

ERNEST CADMAN COLWELL

and

ERIC LANE TITUS

HARPER & BROTHERS PUBLISHERS

NEW YORK

THE GOSPEL OF THE SPIRIT:
A STUDY IN THE FOURTH GOSPEL

FIRST EDITION

H—C

Library of Congress catalog card number: 53-8367

CONTENTS

	Preface	861789	7
Chapter I	Religious Values of the Gospel		11
Chapter II	The Evangelist's Purpose		23
Chapter III	The Evangelist's Method		42
Chapter IV	The Divine Nature of Jesus		71
Chapter V	The Descent of the Spirit		107
Chapter VI	The Revelation of God		142
	Index of Names and Subjects		183
	Index of References		185

PREFACE

This is an interpretation of the Gospel of John. In the first three chapters we have tried to make clear the basis of our interpretation. Chapter I is a statement of the religious values of the book. In Chapters II and III we discuss the author's purpose as it affects his choice of materials, and the author's method of presenting his message as it affects our methods of interpretation.

The central theme of our interpretation lies in two assertions: first, that the doctrine of the Holy Spirit is an important part of the teaching of this Gospel; second, that the Fourth Gospel defines Jesus in terms of revelation. The body of the book tries to present the evidence for these assertions.

We have not tried to discuss all problems that face an interpreter of this Gospel. We believe that those which we avoid have been ably discussed elsewhere. We hope that the present discussion of topics that we regard as important will contribute to an increased understanding of a Gospel whose message we regard as of great value to Christians of our generation.

We are indebted to the following authors and publishers for permission to quote material which we have found useful:

M. R. James, *The Apocryphal New Testament,* published by The Clarendon Press, Oxford, England.

B. W. Bacon, *The Gospel of the Hellenists,* published by Henry Holt & Company, New York.

E. F. Scott, *The Fourth Gospel,* published by Charles Scribner's Sons, New York.

G. H. C. Macgregor, *The Gospel of John,* published by Harper & Brothers, New York.

Edgar J. Goodspeed, *A Life of Jesus,* published by Harper & Brothers, New York.

Beyond this, we have made extensive quotations from *John Defends the Gospel*, published by Willett, Clark, and Company in 1936, which is now out of print.

We are indebted to the International Council of Religious Education for permission to quote several passages from the Revised Standard Version published by Thomas Nelson and Sons. We have indicated the passages where we relied on this translation. Unless otherwise indicated our own translation of the New Testament text has been used.

Ernest Cadman Colwell
Emory University

Eric Lane Titus
School of Religion
University of Southern California

The Gospel of the Spirit

I

Religious Values of the Gospel

It is not accidental that the Fourth Gospel has provided some of the best loved and most deeply religious passages for generations of Christians. A profound concentration of the Christian gospel lies, for example, in the words of John 3:16, "God so loved the world that he gave his only Son, that whoever believes in him should not perish but have eternal life."[1] The Christian who knows little or nothing of critical historical methodology has nevertheless sensed rightly the sublimity and truthfulness of these great words.

It is nevertheless evident that this Gospel is not an easy book to interpret. The layman tends to harmonize its picture of Jesus with that of the Synoptics. But if he is at all thoughtful he will sense a difference in the two presentations. The result is confusion. How, for example, can the Jesus who said, "Why do you call me good? No one is good but God alone," also say, "He who has seen me has seen the Father"?

[1] The Revised Standard Version is used throughout this chapter.

Many ministers as well as laymen are concerned about the proper use of this Gospel. They have learned that it is different from the Synoptics; that it is "not historical." But this negative approach serves only to intensify their problem. The fact is that to many people in our time, "historicity" is the sole criterion of truth. That being the case this "unhistorical" gospel becomes an embarrassment.

It is our conviction that the Fourth Gospel, rightly viewed, is in spite of (or perhaps because of) its "unhistorical" character a book of superlative religious value; that it speaks a message for our time which a more "factual" approach could never do. The latter tends to be static, the former dynamic. This is particularly true of the Fourth Gospel because of its doctrine of the Spirit.

We should perhaps make it plain that this appreciative statement about the Fourth Gospel should not be construed as a minimizing of the importance of the historical Jesus as viewed through Synoptic tradition. There is a contemporary tendency in some quarters to emphasize the living Christ of faith to the virtual exclusion of the Jesus who lived in history. Some go so far as to suggest that if the Jesus of history could be known we might find him quite unattractive; that it is perhaps well that he is shrouded in obscurity. But, they go on to say, this fact should make no difference to our concept of the Christ of faith. Apparently there is, for them, no relationship between the two.

This emphasis on the divine Christ to the virtual exclusion of the historical Jesus constitutes a modern equivalent of the ancient docetic heresy. From the point of view of the Christian church it is a dangerous emphasis for it is a denial of the historic roots of the revelation. Furthermore, it fails to recognize that the Christ concept if it is to be true to the historic roots of the Christian religion must maintain some kind of continuity with the attitude and spirit which characterized Jesus of Nazareth. How easy it is to depart from that attitude and spirit has been demonstrated repeatedly and tragically in Church history! On the other hand it has found its genuine expression in men like St. Francis of Assisi. In such a man the spirit of Jesus and of the living Christ become one. Far from minimizing the importance of the historical Jesus we would want to underscore his significance; the Synoptics must play an important part in this connection.

When this has been said, however, it remains true that the Fourth Gospel has a special relevancy for our generation. Its contribution is due largely to the doctrine of the Spirit which is conceived in dynamic and functional terms. The Gospel writer was aware that the Spirit of God had impinged upon history in the person of Jesus of Nazareth and that the same

(13)

Spirit was creatively and redemptively at work in the Christian fellowship.

The Gospel writer had at his disposal two aspects of the Christian story: the career of Jesus and the living experience of the church. In the story of Jesus the baptism looms as a crucial element. For Mark, Matthew, Luke and the Fourth Gospel writer it had its peculiar significance, associated in each case with divine Spirit and Sonship. From a purely descriptive point of view we might say that the baptism was for Jesus a profound religious experience which gave him a new perspective and a sense of dedication. But it was viewed by his followers as a fresh and decisive inbreaking of creative life; so much so that the early Christians concluded that in this experience of baptism God had acted in a uniquely powerful manner. And the career of Jesus ending in his tragic but ultimately triumphant death proved their point!

The life of the historical Jesus must have been one of great power and beauty: he had achieved a profound dimension of religious awareness and sensitivity, a freedom of spirit in spite of the paralyzing tendencies of a legalistic religious system; he had expressed in his relations with all sorts of men and women an attitude of tender concern; he had faced death with a spirit destined to transform the cross into a symbol of divine redemption. It is probable that Jesus was far more attractive, far more vital, than the literary records could portray. That is why religion must call to its aid music, art, drama and poetry. These alone speak a language capable of expressing at all adequately the superlatively beautiful and meaningful life of Jesus. And it is in part why a Gospel like John came into being.

The impact of this life was strong upon early Christianity. While the fourth evangelist was in no wise attempting to write a biography of Jesus, it is clear that the sheer spirituality of Jesus has made its impression upon his mind. The interim between the crucifixion and the Gospel writer's own day served to make even more luminous the inner spirit of Jesus while the less important and ephemeral aspects of his career dropped away. The evangelist was left with a spiritual increment which he could only describe as Light, Life and Truth. The Light is the light of the world, the Life is eternal life, the Truth is truth which sets men free. Behind such verbal symbols one can discern the idealism of the man of Nazareth; his life with its quality of deathlessness; the freedom of a spiritual maturity. The Jesus of the Fourth Gospel is true to the essential facts of the Jesus of history. For the essential facts of his life are not those related to time and space, to the first century and to Palestine; instead they are timeless and nonprovincial. Of this the Fourth Gospel writer was unmistakably aware: "Blessed are those who have not seen and yet believe."

This spiritual quality incarnated in Jesus was, for our writer, an invasion of history by God himself. The meaning of that enigmatic title ascribed to Jesus, "the Lamb of God" (1:29, 36), is found in relation to this divine initiative. He is *God's lamb.* There is no association here, except verbal and symbolic, with the Passover lamb. Jesus dies at the hour when the Passover lamb was slain but he is not a sacrifice offered to God: *he is God's gift to man.* This title is another way of expressing the fact that Jesus has been sent by God, a view which finds its choicest expression (tinged with poignancy) in the words of 3:16: "God so loved the world that he gave his only Son, that whoever believes in him should not perish but have eternal life."

These and the numerous passages which picture Jesus as God-sent are intended to stress the unity of Jesus with the Father. To be sure, God is still greater than Jesus (14:28), but this is a subordination of position and status not of nature: "He who has seen me has seen the Father" (14:9); "I and the Father are one" (10:30). Jesus is an extension of the Spirit of God into human history.

The life which is bestowed by the Spirit is characterized by deathlessness. The individual who believes in Jesus participates in this eternal life: "Whoever lives and believes in me shall never die" (11:26). In fact, he becomes divine. While this emphasis may be due partly to the Greek idea of *apotheosis,* it is also, and perhaps largely, due to the Christian experience of the resurrection. For whatever external influences played upon the little group of Jesus' followers in the post-crucifixion period, the dominant fact was the overshadowing presence of him who had walked with them in Galilee. There must be posited a direct relation between the one remembered and the one who rose from death to be exalted to the right hand of God.

To say that Christian ideas like eternal life are due to the impact of Hellenistic culture, specifically the dying-and-rising-god concept, is to oversimplify the facts. Certainly, this emphasis helped to consolidate and shape the pattern in which the resurrection faith was presented; it did not produce the faith itself. Rather the concept of resurrection grew out of the *experience* of resurrection. And the experience itself was dependent on the fact of divine life—rich and mighty—dwelling in the Jesus of history.

This spiritual impact of Jesus of Nazareth upon history is indicated by the fact that there were set in motion following his death massive creative emphases like those on freedom and love. It is remarkable how largely the principle of freedom bulks in early Christianity. Reference to it appears in almost if not every book of the New Testament. In most cases it is set forth with the enthusiasm of a new discovery. It gave people like Paul a new perspective on life. It was release, conversion, the religion of the Spirit as opposed to the restricting religion of law.

Surely this emphasis, in itself a gospel, can be traced to Jesus himself. It characterized his whole approach to religion and to all of life. If we were to present examples we could do no better than to quote Mark 2:27: "The sabbath was made for man, not man for the sabbath." This is in principle revolutionary. Or we could suggest the parable of the publican and the Pharisee in Luke 18:10-13:

Two men went up into the temple to pray, one a Pharisee and the other a tax collector. The Pharisee stood and prayed thus with himself, "God, I thank thee that I am not like other men, extortioners, unjust, adulterers, or even like this tax collector. I fast twice a week, I give tithes of all that I get." But the tax collector, standing far off, would not even lift up his eyes to heaven, but beat his breast, saying, "God be merciful to me a sinner!"

But these are only two examples of a spirit and attitude which characterized Jesus' entire ministry. It is this which becomes contagious in the life of the church. It is sounded by Paul like a clarion call around the eastern Mediterranean area. It is at the heart of his gospel. This experience of freedom fascinates the author of the Fourth Gospel also. But with characteristic directness he avoids an exposition on freedom: Jesus himself is the truth which sets men free. He sees clearly that the source of the church's experience of freedom was in Jesus himself. But the source of the divine life of Jesus was the Father. In this manner he traces the priceless heritage of spiritual freedom to God himself.

A second emphasis of the early church was on the gentle side of experience. It is quite remarkable how the vocabulary of Christian writers of the period is graced with words like compassion, mercy, grace, faith, hope, love. It is an invasion of the brutal side of history by the tender to a most amazing degree.

Why did this gentle, sensitizing emphasis arise (along with the affirmation of freedom), at this particular time and in so generous a measure? The answer is found here also in its relation to Jesus of Nazareth. For it was he who was the embodiment of the loving spirit directed both toward God and man. The story of the drama of redemption could not have arisen apart from this great fact. There are other redemption dramas but none with the rich ethical-spiritual dimensions of this one.

The impact of this aspect of the historical Jesus on the Fourth Gospel writer is most evident in the teaching about the new commandment: "This is my commandment, that you love one another as I have loved you. Greater love has no man than this, that a man lay down his life for his friends" (15:12-13). Precisely what love is the writer does not say, but the Christian church would relate it to the supreme act of love in the death of Jesus on the cross.

We can say, then, that two majestic spiritual monuments stand on the field of early Christianity: *freedom* and *love; truth* and *grace.* "The law was given by Moses; grace and truth came through Jesus Christ." They were divinely bestowed through Christ. The revelation through him did not consist of a series of illustrations of ethical conduct. Rather, the ethics of Jesus constituted the natural expression of the divine life within. This is not far from the teaching of Paul in Galatians 5:22-23: "The fruit of the Spirit is love, joy, peace, patience, kindness, goodness, faithfulness, gentleness, self-control." For the Fourth Gospel writer Jesus does not merely teach idealism: he *is* light. Jesus is no mere advocate of moral integrity: he *is* truth. Jesus does not offer a new ethical code: he *is* the way. Jesus does not offer to men an ethical road to life: he *is* life.

This interpretation of Jesus is not untrue to the essential situation. Behind the ethical life of Jesus lay the basic fact of the humble, loving spirit. To have this spirit was what Jesus meant by repentance. It differentiated the publican from the Pharisee, the good Samaritan from the callous priest. It was what made Jesus, Jesus, and the church saw that it was divine in origin and nature. In brief, it was God's spirit operative in history.

Now the attractive thing about this is that it is so relevant an approach for the contemporary church. The gospel of the Spirit looks forward as well as backward. It looks back only to take its cue from the past but its major reference is eternally contemporary. This is explicitly stated in certain passages of the Gospel: "Truly, truly, I say to you, he who believes in me will also do the works that I do; and greater works than these will he do, because I go to the Father" (14:12); "But the Counselor, the Holy Spirit, whom the Father will send in my name, he will teach you all things, and bring to your remembrance all that I have said to you" (14:26). This approach leaves the door wide open to new spiritual insights; the present is the abode of the living Spirit; the backward look is important only as it keeps us true to the genius of the historic revelation. Legalism does not thrive in this climate nor does authoritarianism of any external variety. The gospel of the Spirit is the gospel of creative energy operating within the context of love.

This means that the Fourth Gospel is an interpretation of Jesus. The Evangelist's attention is focused not on the external history of the man Jesus, but on the timeless, universal spiritual values which men had experienced in him. He, too, could have said with Paul: "From now on, therefore, we regard no one from a human point of view; even though we once regarded Christ from a human point of view, we regard him thus no longer" (2 Cor. 5:16). The world of meaning and value which Jesus conveyed transcended his own physical body even as it transcends time and place. In this Gospel the *essential fact* of the Jesus of history becomes the content of the Christ of faith. But this focus of attention on the essential fact obliterates any concern with biographical detail: this is the Gospel of the Spirit.

II

The Evangelist's Purpose

THE earliest Christian communities were one-gospel communities. Before A.D. 125 there is no evidence of the use of more than one gospel in one community.[1] Ignatius of Antioch, for example, who was martyred about A.D. 117, used Matthew alone. When Marcion made the first New Testament collection he used only the Gospel of Luke. In doing this he followed the practice of his contemporaries, for nothing could have seemed more strange to them than the use of two, three or four gospels. It is difficult for us who were born with four stories of Jesus to appreciate their situation. The rivalry between favorites from various localities culminated in the formation of our fourfold group only after a long and bitter struggle. As Harnack long ago pointed out, the strangest thing in the New Testament is

[1] See E. J. Goodspeed, *The Formation of the New Testament* (Chicago, 1925), pp. 33-49. The exceptions are Matthew, Luke, and John. Yet each of them testifies to the existence of a favorite or dominant gospel in his community. For Matthew it was Mark; for Luke, Proto-Luke; for John, Luke.

the presence of four gospels.[2] Embarrassment at the presence of four gospels was felt as early as the second century. Almost as soon as the Roman church accepted our fourfold canon, a young Syrian at Rome blended the four Gospels into one continuous gospel narrative—the *Diatessaron*.

It was both sensible and natural that the author of an early Christian gospel should conceive of his task as the writing of *the* gospel. No one of them planned to write volume two or volume three of the gospel; nor, we can be sure, did any one of them entitle his work "The Second Gospel," "The Third Gospel," etc. "The Gospel of Jesus Christ" (Mark 1:1) indicates the nature of the original titles of our Gospels. The very formality of the opening of Mark is evidence that the author intended his work to be *the* story and not one of many stories.[3] Mark probably had at least one written source, the story of the last week and the resurrection; but no one would insist that he intended his gospel to be read beside this earlier Passion gospel. For the finished work is in itself proof that Mark shaped his sources (oral and written) so as to produce a gospel that could be read without reference to other books or stories. The book written by Mark was a complete and independent story of the gospel of Jesus. As such a sufficient work, it was ac-

[2] Adolf von Harnack, *The Origin of the New Testament* (English translation. New York, 1925), pp. 68-83.

[3] *Ibid.*, p. 72, n. 2.

cepted at Rome, where it served the local community for some time as the Roman gospel.

In the case of Matthew we can see even more clearly the author's conception of his task as the writing of *the* gospel. Part of this increase in clarity comes from our possession of one of his sources, the Gospel of Mark. The possession of a copy of the Gospel by Matthew made the possession of a copy of the Gospel by Mark a superfluous luxury. Matthew incorporates all but about forty verses of the Gospel of Mark.[4] It is for this reason that Matthew's Gospel has been called a fresh, enlarged and revised edition of Mark.[5] Second editions are made to replace first editions, and Matthew would have completely eliminated Mark from Christian libraries if Mark had not already been strongly established in the powerful Roman church.

Matthew supplemented Mark but was in no sense a supplement to Mark. He makes his additions to Mark within the pages of his own Gospel in the effort to produce a better gospel than that by Mark. The success of the effort is shown by the clear preference of the church for Matthew. The preservation of Mark to be read beside Matthew would have seemed incredible to the author of Matthew.

[4] E. J. Goodspeed, *The Story of the New Testament* (Chicago, 1916), p. 61; V. H. Stanton, *The Gospel as Historical Documents* (Cambridge, 1909), II, 324-27.

[5] So, e.g., by F. C. Burkitt, *The Earliest Sources for the Life of Jesus* (London, 1922), p. 97.

Luke also tried to write *the* gospel. That the tone of his comments on previous efforts is depreciatory was obvious to Eusebius:

And when Luke began his composition, he himself set forth the purpose for which he made his arrangement. He shows that the number and diversity of those who too rashly undertake to make an account of the things which He [Jesus] had fulfilled makes it necessary for him [Luke] to free us from the contradictory opinions of the others. Therefore he handed down through his own gospel the accurate account of those things the truth of which he had adequately discovered both from his association and conversation with Paul and from the advantage of his association with the remaining apostles.[6]

Eusebius has skillfully identified the key words and fundamental significance of Luke's prologue. It is because of the existence of a number of divergent gospels that Luke writes *the* gospel so that Theophilus may have a single authority. What Luke tried to give Theophilus was "a security against stumbling or falling" which he could never feel in the confusion caused by the existence of competitive gospels. The presence of several divergent and even contradictory accounts of Jesus' career would disturb and unsettle the believer. To explain Luke's purpose as the writing of another gospel to be used beside "the many" makes his prologue a meaningless *non sequitur*. So conceived, it says, "Since there already are many gospels, I decided to write one more."

---

[6] *Ecclesiastical History*, iii.24, 15.

What he actually says is: "Since there are many gospels, I decided to write the best gospel by combining all the excellences of present gospels; thus I hope to reduce manifold diversity to orderly unity and increase the security of the Christian tradition."[7]

Luke's dependence on Mark is not so extensive as that of Matthew, and Streeter has suggested that Luke combined Mark with another early gospel (Proto-Luke) to form our Third Gospel.[8] This is not to say that Luke expected Mark to rival his new gospel; on the contrary, his combination of Mark with another source which he regarded as at least equally valuable was designed to make the new gospel so much more useful than Mark that the Christian in search of a gospel would inevitably turn away from Mark to Luke.

Professor Cadbury, whose opinion in this area must carry the greatest weight, has claimed that Luke's purpose was the writing of an independent gospel:

I think it is quite wrong to suppose that Luke or even John in writing assumed in the readers a knowledge of earlier gospels. The new work was in each case intended to stand by itself. It is

[7] Professor Cadbury interprets these words as less meaningful and more formal—as part of the formula of a preface. See *The Beginnings of Christianity*, Vol. II, *Prolegomena* II (London, 1922), pp. 489-510.

[8] Canon B. H. Streeter, *The Four Gospels* (first edition, New York, 1925). This Proto-Luke hypothesis has been championed especially by Vincent Taylor, *Behind the Third Gospel: A Study of the Proto-Luke Hypothesis* (Oxford, 1926); *The Gospels, A Short Introduction* (London, 1930); and an article in Theology XIV (1927), pp. 131-64.

we moderns who make the comparison, and only too often we suppose that the author anticipated such comparison, as though John were correcting or supplementing Mark and the other Synoptics, or that Luke were producing a different version to serve for a different community alongside of established and well known predecessors like Mark and Q. Each wrote a work to serve its own purpose, independently and without regard to others. At most an ancient author could hope to be a supplanter.[9]

Further examples of competitive gospels can be found among those which did not become part of the New Testament. In the case of the gospel of the Hebrews it is impossible to decide definitely whether certain fragments are part of this lost gospel or not, but we can be sure of enough to show that it also was a competitive gospel. The Lord's prayer, the sinful woman, the baptism of Jesus, the man with the withered hand and the parable of the talents are some of the familiar sections which are found in quotations from this gospel. That it was written to produce a better and more acceptable gospel which could be used in place of earlier efforts can be seen in such a section as the baptism story, with its insistence upon the sinlessness of Jesus. The description of the first resurrection appearance to James, the brother of the Lord, is another indication of its independ-

[9] H. J. Cadbury, *The Making of Luke-Acts* (New York, 1927), p. 331. He refers to Easton's judgment that Luke expected that his work would be read and understood as a separate work, not to compare or harmonize with other gospels—*The Gospel According to St. Luke* (New York, 1926), p. ix.

ence.[10] The frame is the same, many of the details of the picture are the same; but some have been altered or obliterated and new ones added. The gospel of the Hebrews was another attempt to write *the* gospel.

Later in the second century, another "heretical" competitor produced the gospel of Peter. It was written about A.D. 150 by a Christian who could not accept the doctrine of the incarnation; that Jesus was a God he believed, but he could not believe that he possessed a real physical body. Moreover, he bitterly disliked the Jews. He therefore rewrote the gospel, using all four of our canonical Gospels as sources. In the fragment which describes the trial and death of Jesus, we meet many a familiar detail. Joseph of Arimathea, Herod, Pilate, the two thieves, the guard at the tomb, the myrrh-bearing women, all these play their familiar roles. The difference between this gospel and its sources are no bulkier than those between John and the first three Gospels. Yet it is plain that the author of the gospel of Peter wrote not to supplement but to replace the earlier gospels.[11]

A more recent gospel to be brought to light is preserved in a few fragments at the British Museum and has been published by H. Idris Bell and T. C. Skeat.[12] The papyrus

[10] English version of these sources in M. R. James, *The Apocryphal New Testament* (Oxford: Clarendon Press, 1924), pp. 1-8.

[11] For an English translation, see *Ibid.*, pp. 90-94.

[12] *Fragments of an Unknown Gospel and Other Early Christian Papyri* (London, 1935).

itself has been dated as about A.D. 160. It contains: (a) part of a debate between Jesus and the Jews in Johannine phrases; (b) the healing of a leper; (c) a question about tribute; (d) a very fragmentary account of a nature miracle performed by Jesus as he stood on the bank of the river Jordan. This gospel belongs with such a work as the gospel of Peter, as an attempt to produce a rival to the four. Its dependence on the Synoptics and on John can hardly be questioned, but it is plain that the author uses this material quite freely and supplements it from some other source. The British Museum gospel becomes another item in the list of works written to serve as *the* gospel.

Examples of gospels written to supplement earlier ones exist in the so-called "Infancy Gospels." Here are gospels which were obviously written to fill in the gaps left by the earlier accounts of Jesus' life. These had told little of Jesus' parentage and childhood; the *Protevangelium* and the gospel of Thomas discuss nothing else. They cannot be read apart from at least one of the four Gospels; their *raison d'être* is to supplement. They show us what a noncompetitive, supplementary gospel was like; and they show us clearly that Matthew, Luke and John, as we shall now see, are not of that kind.

The author of the Fourth Gospel undoubtedly used Mark and Luke as his basic sources. He probably used Matthew also, though this is less certain.[13] Since we still possess the books that served John as framework, the task of determining his distinctive purpose is relatively simple. The changes he made by way of omission, addition and transformation should give us the clue as to his dominant distinctive purpose. We use the two adjectives for the simple reason that one fundamental purpose he held in common with the writers of the other Gospels; the evangelistic purpose. All four Gospels were "written that you might believe that Jesus is the Christ, the Son of God, and that—by believing—you might have life through him" (John 20:31). At the trial of Jesus, Luke's Gospel finds its climax in Jesus' acceptance of the accusation that he was "the Christ" and "the Son of God" (22:67-71). The testimony of unbelievers in Mark is used to show that Jesus was the Christ (15:32) and the Son of God (15:39). Matthew diligently employs prophecy to show that Jesus was Messiah, and quotes from Mark the centurion's confession, "Truly this was the Son of God" (27:54). Each

[13] We reject Bultmann's elaborate identification of a Gnostic Sayings-Source and a Miracle-Source; as we do his suggestion that an editor is responsible for many of the agreements with the Synoptics. The possibility that an evangelist may not have achieved complete consistency is made probable by what we find to be true in Paul's thinking, and even in the work of hypothetical editors. Bultmann's editor is supposed to have corrected the eschatology of John to the account in the earlier gospels, but the correction is so slight as to be almost invisible to the ordinary reader of the Gospel. For Bultmann's position, see Rudolf Bultmann, *Das Evangelium des Johannes* (*Kritisch-exegetischer Kommentar über das Neue Testament begrundet von Heinrich August Wilhelm Meyer*) II. durchgesehene Auflage, (Göttingen: Vandenhoeck & Ruprecht, 1950), *passim*; and the review by Kendrick Grobel in *Journal of Biblical Literature*, LIX (1940), pp. 434-36.

THE GOSPEL OF THE SPIRIT

author wrote as he did so that the reader would accept these titles for Jesus. Any contrast between John and the Synoptics on this basis is a false contrast.[14] The only real difference in this respect is that what the authors do for Jesus in the Synoptics Jesus does for himself in John.

But like most authors before and since, our evangelists wrote with mixed motives and thus produced the individuality that keeps them distinct in their common setting. The peculiar motives of John can, therefore, be determined not by focusing attention on John 20:31, but by a thorough survey of the changes which he made in his sources.

Most of these changes are unnoticed by the reader of the fourfold Gospel because they are omissions. If we are to see the Gospel of John clearly, we must first of all see what

[14] This unfortunate contrast between John as "theological" and the Synoptics as "historical" was given a wide vogue by Professor Scott's invaluable study of John, *The Fourth Gospel: Its Purpose and Theology* (Edinburgh: T. & T. Clark, 1906), pp. 2 f. It is echoed in interpretations of the Fourth Gospel; e.g., M. E. Lyman, *The Fourth Gospel and the Life of Today* (New York: 1931), pp. 10-27. But this gap between John and the Synoptics has, to a large degree, been closed by the gospel study of the last generation. The work of Wrede and the *Formgeschichtliche* school in Germany, the work of B. W. Bacon, especially *The Beginnings of the Gospel Story* (New Haven, 1909), and of S. J. Case in *The Evolution of Early Christianity* (Chicago, 1914), and *Jesus: A New Biography* (Chicago, 1927), especially Chapters I, II and VIII of the latter, has moved John and the Synoptists closer together. A stimulating study of the gospels by an Oxford scholar, R. H. Lightfoot, *History and Interpretation in the Gospels* (New York, 1935), abandoned the false antithesis between the historical Synoptics and the religious John. But it is the Synoptics, and not John, that moved. We now realize that the fundamental interest of the Synoptics, as of John, was a religious interest. It would be an incredible anachronism to say today, as Scott did, that the Synoptics are fundamentally different from John in that their chief aim was fidelity to historical tradition, and the recording of facts.

(32)

THE EVANGELIST'S PURPOSE

is not there. Professor Clayton R. Bowen forcefully indicated the extent of the omissions. The author, he pointed out, nowhere

uses the words pity, mercy, compassion, nor suggests the quality; nowhere brings in the poor (only 12:5 f.), or the rich; nowhere a publican, a sinner, a widow, a child, a scribe, a Sadducee; nowhere mentions any of the Herods, or Gentiles; no Tyre or Sidon, no Mount of Olives; no unclean demoniacs or reference to their cleansing; no repentance and no forgiveness of sin, neither the words nor the ideas; no *prayer* or praying ("ask" and "beg" occur), no *gospel,* no *preaching,* no apostle (the word in 13:16 is in another sense); no faith, no hope, no wisdom; no *parable,* and most amazingly, no Kingdom of God (3:3-5 being the one exception)....[15]

To this list it may be added that in John there is no genealogy, no birth of Jesus, no birth of the Baptist, no wise men or shepherds, no flight to Egypt, no slaughter of the innocents, no visit of the boy Jesus to the temple, no actual baptism of Jesus, no future judgment, no second Messianic coming, no room for Pentecost, no sons of Zebedee, no fishermen, no institution of the Lord's Supper, no marvels at the death of Jesus, no gradual revelation of Jesus, no Messianic secret, no women companions on his travels, no earthly life of humiliation, no tribute to John the Baptist by anyone, no

[15] "Comments on the Fourth Gospel," *Anglican Theological Review* XII (1929-1930), p. 230.

repudiation of the title "good" by Jesus, no accusation against Jesus by his family, no inquiring embassy from the imprisoned Baptist, no healing of a leper, no stilling of a storm at sea, no real betrayal of Jesus, no transfiguration, no kiss by Judas or thirty pieces of silver, no mission of the twelve or the seventy, no beatitudes, no Lord's prayer, no "First Commandment," no exhortation to self-denial (except for other Christians), no cursing of the fig tree, no agony in Gethsemane, no penitence on Peter's part for his denial, no Simon of Cyrene to carry the cross, no mocking or taunting of Jesus on the cross, no cry from the cross: "My God, My God, why have you forsaken me?", no use of Aramaic by Jesus, no loud cry at the death of Jesus, no fasting, no temptation of Jesus, no lament over Jerusalem, no ascension.

Most of these omissions were consciously and deliberately made by the author. Some few items may have been omitted as relatively unimportant, but the majority were exscinded because they did not fit in with the author's conception of Jesus or with his purpose in writing the Gospel.[16] One who omitted so ruthlessly and in many respects so consistently could not have planned to put his book beside another whose presence would nullify this careful work.

[16] "The omission of so much Synoptic material by our evangelist is accounted for by his purpose"—W. Heitmueller, "Das Johannes-Evangelium," *Die Schriften des Neuen Testamentes* (3rd ed., Goettingen, 1918), IV, 26.

The paucity of new material stands in the way of the assumption that John wrote to supplement the Synoptics from some other source. For, although there is considerable addition in minor detail, especially in the Passion narrative, there is not as much significant addition as might be expected. The list of additions to the narrative is quite brief. It contains the numerous visits to Jerusalem, Jesus' success in Samaria, the wedding feast at Cana, the sick man *at Bethesda,* the man *born* blind, Lazarus, the footwashing, and Jesus' demonstration of power at the arrest.[17] 861789

In the teaching sections the additions lie in that area of thinking which is usually called Gnostic. Jesus is The One Sent that the readers might know God and his Messenger. Knowing is the most important function in the book, and the Gospel thus acquires an appearance of learnedness. But the knowledge is fundamentally religious and not intellectual; the intellectuality is no more than an attractive cloak for Jesus. He is a god. As such he comes as light into darkness, life into death; a god from above; he is sent into the world below that man might know him or not know him, might believe him or not. In vocabulary and idea this is a new teaching—new, that is, to a Christian gospel, but already familiar to the religious syncretism of the day. The Jesus of John teaches in a terminology and thought world

[17] *Ibid.*

unknown to the earlier evangelists. That is not the supplementation of the gospel, but its transformation.[18]

The fourth evangelist not only omits and adds, he also makes drastic changes in what he uses. His independence in the reshaping of Synoptic tradition is shown in his treatment of the baptism of Jesus. The stirring exhortations to repentance with which the Baptist addresses his audience in each of the earlier gospels are replaced by the Baptist's emphatic confession that he is a religious leader of no significance.

In fact, John cannot use Synoptic material without changing it. A comparison of any of the passages urged as agreements between John and the other evangelists will make clear this fact. Nowhere does John follow the Marcan account more closely than in the story of the feeding of the five thousand and its sequel, the walking on the sea. Yet in Mark, Jesus retires to the mountain after the feeding to pray; while in John, he goes up the mountain to escape the

---

[18] The weakness of the "supplement" claim is apparent in its statement by Eusebius (*Ecclesiastical History*, iii.24, 11-13):

"They say, therefore, that the Apostle John, being asked to do it for this reason, gave in his gospel an account of the period which had been omitted by the earlier evangelists, and of the deeds done by the Savior during that period; that is, of those which were done before the imprisonment of the Baptist. . . . John accordingly in his gospel records the deeds of Christ which were performed before the Baptist was cast into prison, but the other three evangelists mentioned the events which happened after that time. One who understands this can no longer think that the gospels are at variance with one another."

But to any but the most superficial survey, it is plain that the most striking additions, in fact the bulk of the Gospel of John, follow the imprisonment of the Baptist.

demands of a group of revolutionists who want him to head their rebellion. In John, as in the earlier gospels, one of the disciples is identified as Satan after Peter's confession, but it is Judas and not Peter. In the Synoptics, Jesus' teaching is centered around the two great commandments; in John these are replaced by a "new" commandment (13:34 f). "In saying 'new,' he has made the former old; but that which is made old and has become infirm is about to vanish."[19]

The healing of the nobleman's son (4:46-54), is an excellent illustration of his use of Synoptic material. A similar miracle story appears in Luke 7:1-10 and Matthew 8:5-13. The use of the story by John is probably suggested by the climax of the story in Luke 7:9, "I tell you I have not found such faith as this even in Israel." Such faith is defined by the Lucan narrative as faith that Jesus could perform a miracle at a distance. That he did so is what occasions Jesus' exclamation over the quality of the man's faith. But in John the excellence of the man's faith is that it does not rest upon signs. He believes without seeing signs. It is true that Jesus said, "Unless you see signs and marvels, you will not believe," but the man immediately indicates his belief. The story, then, is a means of exemplifying the highest possible quality of faith. This is meant by the author of the

[19] Hebrews 8:13, quoted in this connection by Hans Windisch, *Johannes und die Synoptiker* (Leipzig, 1926), p. 118.

Fourth Gospel to stand in contrast to the faith of the Jews in Jerusalem and in Galilee who believed on Jesus because they saw signs (2:23, 4:45). Jesus' commendation of the excellence of the man's faith would be as applicable in John as in Luke, but the quality of his faith is entirely different, for it is based on a superior reason.

There are other differences in this story between John on the one hand and Matthew and Luke on the other. They may be classified as follows. In the first place, some of the new material consists of cross-references. The story begins with a reference to Cana in Galilee where Jesus had made the water wine (2:1-11). In 4:47 there is another cross-reference in the statement that Jesus had come from Judea to Galilee. This refers to the preceding section (4:43). A similar cross-reference occurs in 4:54: "This was now the second sign that Jesus did when he had come from Judea to Galilee" (R.S.V.). This combines the reference both to Cana and the trip in a literary cross-reference. This kind of material constitutes one new element in the story.

In the second place, the Johannine story includes details which, whether they were added by the evangelist or in the course of oral transmission, make it a better story. The rank of the father is increased; instead of a centurion, as in the other Gospels, he is one of the king's officials, a nobleman. Another change is in the relationship of the one who is healed: he is the official's *son,* not his *slave.* A further change occurs in the time of the healing. In the Fourth Gospel it takes place the exact moment when Jesus spoke to the father. The story in the later Gospel ends with the statement of the conversion of the nobleman and his whole household. This is an unusual statement in the Gospel but is fairly common in the Acts narrative.[20]

All of these changes are part of a general toning up of the story. This is what happens to stories that are repeated over and over again; they become more dramatic, more interesting and better stories. This tendency applies to the early Christians as well as to others. We do not know the exact form in which the fourth evangelist received the story, but most of the changes referred to would be congenial to him in terms of the content of the rest of the Gospel. This is underscored by the fact that the peculiarly Jewish elements in the story have all vanished. In Matthew's account (8:11-21) there is the typical Jewish end-of-the-world teaching that does not reappear in John. Luke's tribute to the faith of the man (7:9) is also a tribute to the priority of Israel in matters of faith. "I have not found such faith as this even in Israel" is to imply that the natural home for faith is Israel. But that saying is absent from John.

At what point in the transmission of this story these

---

[20] Acts 16:15, 31, 34; 18:8.

Jewish elements were removed it is impossible for us to know, but it is reasonable to conclude that if they had vanished from the story before the fourth evangelist used it, he would find the story more appealing for that reason. If they were still there when he first heard it, he would conclude that they were distortions and corruptions that were added by people who did not know the full truth. He would therefore correct them.

Now it is interesting to note that if the details mentioned are removed from the story there is nothing left but the skeleton of the narrative which appears in the other Gospels. The basic source of this could have been either the story as it appears in Matthew or the story as it appears in Luke or in some third form similar to these but not containing any new material. The author of the Fourth Gospel could have produced the story out of the material in Luke or Matthew.

All this omission, addition and change makes the Gospel of John a new gospel. It shows plainly that the evangelist's purpose was to write the only gospel necessary to a knowledge of Jesus as the light and life of the world. But, when the purpose of the evangelist has been defined as the writing of *the* gospel, the definition of his purpose has been begun, but no more. What were the varying interests that fused together in his purpose? Why did he choose what he did from the wealth of Christian tradition about Jesus that came down to him? Part of the answer lies in the fact that John and his audience were Christians of more culture than those who listened to Paul and those who wrote and read the earlier gospels. But there were other reasons which we shall examine at length in later chapters. In the meantime, it is necessary to make clear the method employed by the Gospel writer as it affects our method of interpretation.

III

The Evangelist's Method

E. F. SCOTT once wrote that "the Fourth Gospel, in outward appearance so unstudied and spontaneous, is in reality a work of complex art."[1] No serious student of the Gospel can take issue with that judgment. Failure to appreciate it results in gross misrepresentations and the loss of many valuable religious insights which the book has to offer. A knowledge of the art of the Gospel through an analysis of its distinctive features makes possible a statement of methods which may help toward a more intelligent interpretation.

1. The point of departure is the author's use of sources. These were primarily Paul's letters and the Synoptic Gospels. He also made use of the book of Acts, though this is not generally conceded. He probably had access to other tradition not now available. In any case the fourth evangelist used his sources with the utmost freedom. His interest lay primarily not in the events described but in their symbolic

[1] *The Fourth Gospel, Its Purpose and Theology*, p. 22.

value indicative of the eternal significance of Jesus. This being the case, it was possible for him not only to use sources which dealt with the career of Jesus but also those which reflected developments within the church. Consequently, Pauline ideas are read back into the mind of Jesus, likewise events of the book of Acts. From his vantage-point in the second century the evangelist sees these developments as latent in the life of Jesus. This is not a distortion inasmuch as the total meaning of Jesus was not circumscribed by the few months or years of his so-called public ministry. His life found more complete fulfillment in the early church; indeed, it appears that even in the twentieth century the story is far from being concluded as the implications of his life for our larger and more complex world unfold.

2. A striking literary device is the use made of "stupid characters." Throughout the Gospel there are individuals or groups who misunderstand the true import of Jesus' words. Their ignorance serves as a foil for the spiritual utterances of Jesus. Examples are found in the Nicodemus story of chapter three where Nicodemus fails to understand Jesus because he operates on the essentially physical level of experience, whereas Jesus is thinking in terms of the spirit; in the Samaritan woman incident of chapter four, where the woman fails to get beyond the idea of the water in Jacob's well, whereas Jesus is speaking of the water of life;

in the story of the feeding of the five thousand in chapter six, where the Jews who are physically satiated cannot appreciate that Jesus' words about bread can mean anything other than material food; in the account of the giving of the new commandment in chapter thirteen where even his disciples fail to understand his reference to "going away."

This feature of the Gospel is closely related to the fact that within a given narrative the development is from the crassly physical to the highly spiritual concept. Indeed, it seems to be the way in which the Gospel itself is constructed: the progression of thought is from the witness of John, to the witness of the signs, to the witness of the words of Jesus and of the Father, to the witness of the Spirit itself in the experience of the church.

3. Another example of the art of John is found in the subtle use of verbal symbols. The author uses ambiguous words with telling effect. Usually the ambiguous word contains an obviously physical significance and a secondary, spiritual connotation. Invariably the Jews seize the "lower" meaning permitting Jesus to make a solemn pronouncement in terms of the "higher" idea involved.[2] Sometimes the ambiguity is inherent in the word itself as in the case of *anōthen* (meaning "again" or "from above"; 3:3); at other times it

[2] See Bultmann's note in his commentary in the Meyer series, *Das Evangelium des Johannes*, p. 95, n. 2, and in the *Ergänzungsheft*, p. 19.

is involved in a term which lends itself to symbolism. Examples of the latter are "bread," "water," "life," "temple."

The use of apparently synonymous words is a similar feature of the Gospel. Superficially observed they appear to serve merely for literary variety, but in many instances go far beyond this simple purpose.

4. The characters of the Gospel present a particularly interesting feature. Some of them have no Synoptic counterparts; for example, Nathanael, Nicodemus, the Beloved Disciple, Lazarus. They figure in the account not because they were historical personages, but because they are representative types.

5. The gospel is highly dramatic in character. This feature of the work is largely missed if viewed as history or interpreted through the Synoptic Gospels. The Gospel is not a compilation as are the Synoptics, but a closely knit composition. This makes possible intensely dramatic scenes such as when Pilate brings Jesus before the mob and says, "Behold the man!" (19:5).

The foregoing aspects of the Fourth Gospel do not exhaust the list of literary devices employed by the author. They do, however, constitute the more important ones. Each of these categories leads to a corresponding principle for guidance in the interpretation of the Gospel. These will be stated in the following paragraphs. In each case application will be made to sample passages from the Gospel.

1. The interpreter of the Fourth Gospel must seek to isolate the source of a given passage; he must note the original setting and purpose of the source material, also changes in the new context, omissions from and additions to the source. In his attempt to isolate the source, he must remember that the author is interested in material for its symbolic value. This means that he will take an idea or a combination of ideas and work them into an entirely new literary arrangement to suit his own purposes. The story of Lazarus will illustrate most of these features.

In the Synoptics, Lazarus is found only in the parable of the rich man and Lazarus (Luke 16:19-31). The point of the Lucan parable is to show that even if one were to rise from the dead, the Jews would not believe. The Gospel writer demonstrates this by having Lazarus actually rise from the dead. The raising of Lazarus is the last and greatest of the signs and exhausts all possibilities of the Jews believing. In fact, scholars speak of the raising of Lazarus as the "inciting incident" of the Fourth Gospel, taking the place, in that respect, of the cleansing of the temple in the Synoptic accounts. In order to give Lazarus a historical reference, the writer superimposes him upon the Mary and Martha family situation as found in the tenth chapter of

Luke. Jesus, by raising Lazarus, demonstrates that he is the Resurrection and the Life, but even this last and greatest of the signs fails to convince the Jews. The remainder of the Gospel is the tragic sequel showing the attendant circumstances of unbelief; tragic, that is, for the Jews in their failure to recognize essential and spiritual life.

The evangelist's use of sources is illustrated further by his treatment of Pauline ideas. It is very generally held that Paul's letters are an important source for the Gospel of John. There is, however, an important qualification which needs to be made on the relation of the Fourth Gospel to Paul. While it is true that the Johannine Gospel shows dependence upon Pauline thought, it is equally true that there are large areas of Pauline thought for which the Gospel writer's mind shows no affinity. The fact is that the Gospel materials suggest both attraction and aversion to the thought of Paul.

The areas of dependence have been presented ably elsewhere so that for purposes of this study it will be necessary only to indicate them without argument. They are (1) the concept of the Spirit, (2) the idea of the new creation, (3) the resurrection emphasis. In each of these cases, however, the Evangelist makes modifications according to his own religious genius. For him the Spirit is the dominant idea without the complications of a transactionalism or an imminent eschatology. The idea of the new creation is conceived by the Fourth Gospel in dynamic terms quite apart from the sacramentalism of Paul. Resurrection, for the evangelist, is conceived in terms of a present depth dimension of life with no relation to an end-of-the-age transformation. In general, it can be said that the Gospel writer's mind is attracted to those areas of Paul's thought which are embraced by the rather elusive term "mystical."

The fact of omission assumes an increased importance when it is remembered that the Fourth Gospel, in all probability, comes from the period when the Pauline corpus was at the height of its influence in the first part of the second century.

Transactionalism. There is in Paul's letters a large area of thought which is sometimes indicated by the word "transactionalism." It has to do with Paul's concept of the function of the cross. It represents an attempt on the part of the Jewish Paul to explain the difficult fact of the crucifixion: the cross is the substitute for Torah as a way of righteousness. When writing from this point of view Paul becomes rationalistic, argumentative, uninspiring. One might venture to guess that this interpretation of the means of divine acquittal held in leash the mighty upsurge of spiritual power which he had experienced in his greatest religious moment and which needed other categories for natural expression.

(48)

The fourth evangelist, apparently, felt no attraction to this aspect of Paul's thought for it is absent from his Gospel. For him the death of Jesus far from being a transaction was the divine mechanism for the universalizing of the gospel: the crucifixion is the breaking of the crucible containing the precious ointment of the Spirit. Had it not taken place the essential Life that was in Jesus would have remained local and temporal; now it has become universal and eternal. Pauline transactionalism has no appeal to his poetic, mystical, imaginative mind.

Eschatology. The eschatological emphasis bulks large in the thought of Paul. In this he is at one with the Jewish emphasis and with that of the primitive Christian community. Paul apparently felt it necessary to retain the eschatological point of view in spite of the fact that his experience of the indwelling Christ gave him the essential element in salvation. Nevertheless, he was (understandably) so intimately involved in the thought pattern of his group that he retained the notion of the imminent inbreaking of God as necessary to the consummation of salvation. The present condition of the justified man or of the one in whom Christ dwells is a foretaste and a guarantee of what can only be fully realized at the end of the age.

There is wide agreement among scholars that John repudiates the eschatological outlook which characterized the Christian community as represented, for example, by the primitive church, Paul and the Synoptics. The so-called vestiges of eschatology in the Fourth Gospel appear to us to be references to the crucifixion. The "last day" of this Gospel is the all-important day of the crucifixion. However that may be, it remains true that John has interpreted the parousia in terms of the immanent spiritual Presence in the community. Like Marcion after him, the fourth evangelist feels an aversion to *phases* of Jewish thought if not to Jewish thought in general. Certainly the content of the eschatological expectation was too physical in character for one with his entirely spiritual concern.

Sacramentalism. Almost certainly Paul entertained a sacramental concept of baptism and the Lord's Supper. His concept of the new creation, dying with Christ in baptism and rising with him to newness of life, represents a decided break with Judaism. In this respect Paul is nearer to the Mysteries than he is to the religion of his fathers.

Now the Fourth Gospel writer employs language similar to that of Paul, although the word *anōthen* (3:3) in its higher meaning signifies "from above" (i.e., of the Spirit), rather than "again."[3] Nevertheless, the whole emphasis of

[3] The Gospel writer, of course, employs it deliberately because of its double meaning.

the Gospel is that men can become "new creations"; in fact they become divine beings.

How does this transformation take place? Is it the result of a sacramental act? The question is sometimes answered in the affirmative. It is our opinion that this is not the case. For one thing, the absence of the Supper, as such, with the substitution of the lesson in humility suggests otherwise. The account of the feeding of the five thousand can hardly be pressed here since the discourse on the Bread of Life ends with an affirmation of the spiritual nature of what has been said. Furthermore, water baptism is minimized; it is John's baptism and that is inferior to Spirit baptism. A sacramentalist could scarcely say that the Spirit, like the wind, "blows where it wills and you do not know where it comes from or where it goes." The sacramentalist knows exactly when and where the Spirit operates: through the sacramental act itself.

No, John repudiates sacramentalism, Pauline or otherwise![4] Apparently, it is not congenial to his religious outlook. Why? Because it violated his dynamic concept of religion. For him the Spirit is functionally and dynamically

---

[4] On the nonsacramental character of the body of the gospel see Bultmann, *op. cit.*, p. 98, n. 2-3; pp. 174 f.; p. 359, n. 4. Bultmann's appeal to an ecclesiastical redactor as explanation of the few "sacramental" passages seems unnecessary to us. An understanding of the nonsacramental nature of these very passages is gained (as we argue later in this chapter) by following the progression of thought to the end.

present in the church's experience leading its members into ever-enlarging experiences of awareness of meaning and value. The sacramental view of religion is consequently too mechanical for him to embrace it. We would go so far as to say that the Fourth Gospel represents a reaction to an increasing suppression of spontaneous religious experience through the substitution of an *ex opere operato* sacramental ritual.

We have not attempted here to indicate all of the areas of omission with respect to John's use of Pauline thought but rather to suggest the more important ones. A recognition of the fact that while the Fourth Gospel is indebted to Paul, it also fails at points to be so, helps to shed light on its author's use of sources. He used Paul, not slavishly but with discrimination. The fact that he rejects sacramentalism suggests that his nonuse of thoroughly Jewish concepts is not merely because they are Jewish, for sacramentalism also is non-Jewish. It is evident that he is averse to all physical, mechanical phases of religious expression. In his use of sources generally, the mind of John fastens, almost instinctively, on those concepts which lend themselves to a dynamic approach to the religious life.

2. The movement within a given narrative means that the authentic meaning of a passage is to be gained, as a rule, *only by following the progression of thought to the end.*

Any intermediate pronouncement is of inferior worth and to seize upon it as the message of the passage results in erroneous interpretation. An intermediate pronouncement may indeed represent the level of religious insight which the evangelist finds characteristic of the contemporary church, but he advances beyond this to what he considers to be the ideal level. Hence, the "clincher" or "punch line" comes at the end. The only exception to this rule is found in the story of the raising of Lazarus, and this is because in contrast to the other narratives involving signs, the miracle comes at the end rather than the beginning.

This principle is illustrated by the story of the feeding of the five thousand (6:1-65). The first part of the story deals with the miracle itself with its consequent result in a kind of belief on the part of the people: "This is indeed the prophet who is to come into the world."[5] The writer, by using the term "the prophet," suggests that there is not real belief present here, for while in verse fifteen it is indicated that Jesus saw that they were about to come and make him king, the sequel shows that their desire was superficially based. The writer is constantly injecting into the narrative belief which is not real, that is, not abiding. This is probably due to two factors with which he had to deal; on the one hand his picture of Jesus as a divine being *ought* to result in

[5] The Biblical quotations in this section are from the Revised Standard Version.

the recognition of his true nature; on the other hand he was confronted with the historical fact of the Jewish rejection.

The story of the walking on the sea, at first glance foreign to the account of the feeding of the five thousand, actually serves two purposes. For one thing, it acts as a transition to the dialogue with the Jews (verses 25 ff.), but more important still it underscores the ultimate teaching of the whole section: the spiritual nature of Jesus. This idea, however, has not yet been made explicit. Jesus' presence on the other side of the sea is for the Jews merely a source of wonderment: "Rabbi, when did you come here?" Jesus confirms this view of their essentially physical orientation by his words: "You seek me, not because you saw signs, but because you ate your fill of the loaves" (6:26).

This reference to the loaves leads to the idea of the heavenly bread, not yet equated with Jesus, but placed more in the category of the manna in the wilderness. This, in turn, leads to the eager request: "Give us this bread always."

A further step is taken when Jesus explicitly states: "I am the bread of life," and "I have come down from heaven." This results in the discussion among the Jews regarding the origin of Jesus. They state what they know well enough; he is the son of Joseph and they know his father and mother. This lack of spiritual discernment calls for clarification by Jesus leading to the crucial statement: "I am the living bread which came down from heaven; if any one eats of this bread, he will live forever; and the bread which I shall give for the life of the world is my flesh" (6:51).

For the Jews, still physically oriented, this is an impossibility: "How can this man give us his flesh to eat?" This leads to the categorical statement by Jesus: "Unless you eat the flesh of the Son of man and drink his blood, you have no life in you." It is to be noted that here for the first time "blood" appears along with "flesh." This is obviously a reference to the sacramental meal of the Christian church. From then on the Jews disappear from the narrative and the disciples take their place.

The next step is the high point of the account. Jesus' statement regarding the eating of his flesh and the drinking of his blood caused his disciples to be offended: "This is a hard saying; who can listen to it?" Jesus, in response, makes the final statement in which he clarifies the symbolism employed: "It is the spirit that gives life, the flesh is of no avail; the words that I have spoken to you are spirit and life" (6:63).

This last statement is the "clincher," throwing light on all that had gone before. Now we see that Jesus has been leading the disbelieving Jews from one level of thought to another, but their physically oriented minds cannot go beyond the literal meaning of the verbal symbols. It is only when the final pronouncement is made that the spiritual nature of the message is made clear.

How important it is to recognize this progression of thought within the narrative is underscored by the fact that interpretations of the passage frequently find the core of its meaning in the intermediate reference to the flesh and the blood. If one is grounded on this section of the narrative he is left with no alternative than pure sacramentalism. This is the error of a verse-by-verse interpretation of the Fourth Gospel. To avoid this error, one must see the section in its entirety; he must follow the movement of the writer from one idea and symbol to the next and note the crucial, clinching idea. Anything short of this must inevitably lead to a distortion of the meaning of the writer. In the passage discussed, the final pronouncement is in effect a repudiation of sacramentalism, the symbols employed in the intermediate stages of the account being convenient literary vehicles for the development of thought.

This formal arrangement of dialogue is characteristic of the Fourth Gospel. Conversations are for the most part unnatural. A few examples may be stated as follows:

2:13-22 Occasion: What sign have you to show us for doing this? 2:18.
Cryptic remark: Destroy this temple, etc., 2:19.

Stupid remark: It has taken forty-six years to build this temple, etc., 2:20.

Development: 2:21, 22.

4:7-26 Occasion: Give me a drink, etc., 4:7-9.

Cryptic remark: He would have given you living water, 4:10.

Stupid remark: You have nothing to draw with and the well is deep, etc., 4:11-12.

Cryptic remark: Everyone who drinks of this water will thirst again, 4:13-14.

Stupid remark: Sir, give me this water, etc., 4:15.

Development: 4:16-26.

8:31-59 Occasion: Many believed in him, 8:30.

Cryptic remark: The truth will make you free, 8:32.

Stupid remark: We have never been in bondage to anyone, 8:33.

Development: 4:34-38.

Cryptic remark: You do the things which you heard from your father, 8:38.

Stupid remark: Our father is Abraham, 8:39.

Development: 8:39-41.

Cryptic remark: You do the works of your father, 8:41.

Stupid remark: We were not born of fornication, 8:41.

Development: 8:42-47.

Cryptic remark: He who is of God hears the words of God, 8:47.

Stupid remark: You are a Samaritan and have a demon, 8:48.

Development: 8:49-51.

Cryptic remark: He will never see death, 8:51.

> Stupid remark: Are you greater than our Father Abraham who died? 8:52.
>
> Development: 8:53-56.
>
> Cryptic remark: Abraham rejoiced to see my day, 8:56.
>
> Stupid remark: You are not yet fifty years old, etc., 8:57.
>
> Development: 8:58-59.

3. The author's use of verbal symbols calls for great caution in interpretation and translation. The use of *anōthen* (3:3), is a case in point. The Gospel writer finds it valuable because it means either "again" or "from above." Nicodemus, a type of the physically oriented Jew, seizes upon the lower meaning: "How can a man be born when he is old?" This gives Jesus the opportunity to expound on the other meaning of the word; namely, birth from above, i.e., of the Spirit. It is a literary device resulting in the creation of a teaching situation. An accurate translation would call for an exact English equivalent in terms of ambiguity of meaning.[6]

The same thing is found in 2:23-24 where the verb πιστεύειν ("to believe") occurs in successive verses with quite different meaning: The Jews believed on Jesus, but Jesus did not trust himself to the Jews. The author of the Gospel knew that a secondary meaning of πιστεύειν is "to entrust oneself

[6] We suggest as an example the term "regenerated" as a substitute for the phrase "born *anōthen*," since it carries both the literal, physical meaning and a secondary theological connotation. But this suggestion has illustrative value only since it would scarcely suffice in a formal translation. In the translation it would be advisable to render *anōthen* as "again," the meaning Nicodemus is supposed to get, and indicate in a footnote the second meaning, upon which the author intends that Jesus shall expound.

to" when the pronoun repeats the subject. He used it because he wanted to focus attention on the nature of the belief.

In 3:5-8 there is a play on the word "spirit":

Amen, amen, I say to you, except one is begotten of water and spirit he is not able to enter into the Kingdom of God. That which is begotten of flesh is flesh and that which is begotten of spirit is spirit. Do not be surprised because I said to you, "It is necessary to be begotten over again." The wind (πνεῦμα) blows (πνεῖ) where it wills and you hear the sound of it but you do not know where it comes from and where it is going. So is everyone who is begotten of the spirit (ἐκ τοῦ πνεύματος).

Here is one of the clearest examples of double meaning in the Gospel. "Spirit" and "wind" are the same word (πνεῦμα).

In 3:14 there is another play on words: "As Moses lifted up the serpent in the desert so it is necessary for the Son of man to be lifted up." The word ὕψωσεν ("lifted up") also means "exalted." It passes from the physical and concrete meaning to the abstract and figurative. Jesus must be lifted up on the cross as the snake was lifted up in the desert. But he must also be exalted, manifest his glory. The Fourth Gospel writer has both of these ideas in mind. He means to suggest that crucifixion is a lifting up, a glorification and exaltation of Jesus. The cross is an elevator that lifts Jesus to heaven. It demonstrates his divine nature.[7]

[7] Other passages which contain words with double meanings are: 1:14; 2:4; 7:6; 8:28, 50; 9:33, 39-41; 10:7; 11:4, 11-22.

4. The characters of the Gospel must be studied in terms of their symbolic value. Whatever else he may be, the Beloved Disciple is a symbol of the ideal disciple and so of the church. Judas, on the other hand, is a type of the unbelieving Jews. It is difficult to escape the impression that Philip is equated with Philip the evangelist of the Acts account. Because of his part in the Samaritan mission (Acts 8:5 ff.), and because of his contact with the Ethiopian official (Acts 8:26-40), he becomes the ideal person through whom to introduce the Greeks (John 12:20-22). It is one way of saying that the future universality of the gospel is already latent in Jesus, for immediately after the reference to the Greeks Jesus makes the pronouncement as to the function of his death: "Amen, Amen, I say to you except the grain of wheat, when it falls into the earth, dies, it remains alone, but if it dies it bears much fruit" (12:24).

A good example of this symbolism is found in the story of the Samaritan woman (John 4:1-42). There can be little doubt that the Samaritan woman is a type of the Samaritan people. But why does the evangelist use a *woman* as a symbol? Who are the five husbands of the woman? Who is the woman's present consort? Why does he affirm that the Samaritans worship "what they do not know?" These, and other questions, have received no adequate explanation.

It would appear that the source of the Johannine account

is the story of the Samaritan mission in Acts 8:4-24. A review of the story follows: Philip goes into "a city of Samaria" and preaches the message about Christ. He also carries on a ministry of exorcism and healing. As a result there is "much joy in that city." Simon, the magician, is then introduced as one who amazed the nation of Samaria. He is characterized by the people as "that power of God which is called Great." It is his ability to work magic which amazes them. However, the preaching of Philip is so successful that the Samaritans believe and even Simon himself believes and remains with Philip. Then Peter and John come to Samaria from Jerusalem and give to them the Holy Spirit through the laying on of hands. Simon covets this power for himself and offers the disciples money for it. To this Peter replies: "Your silver perish with you, because you thought you could obtain the gift of God with money!"

If we compare the Johannine acount with this several similarities appear. In this case Jesus on his way through Samaria comes "to a city of Samaria, called Sychar." This is the same wording as in the Acts account with the exception that in John the city is identified. In Acts Simon attempts to purchase "the gift of God" (the Holy Spirit), with money (Acts 8:20). In John, Jesus tells the Samaritan woman that if she knew "the gift of God" she could obtain "living water" (i.e., the Spirit), by merely asking him for it (4:10).

Thus, the phrase "the gift of God" is used in both accounts and in each instance refers to the Spirit. In the Johannine story, the disciples go into the city to buy food. Later in the narrative they offer some to Jesus but he replies that he has food to eat that they do not know. This may be a way of saying that the food which Jesus possesses is not something that can be bought; it is the priceless gift of the Spirit.

But the central problem is the identification of the five husbands, and particularly of the woman's consort. In order for us to examine this problem it will be necessary first to review the major aspects of the Simon Magus tradition in the early period.

The Acts account provides the earliest reference to Simon. But additional early information is obtained from the writings of Justin Martyr. Justin says that Simon was worshiped as a god both in Samaria and in Rome. He also informs us that he took about with him a woman named Helena who had formerly been a prostitute. Justin probably looked upon Simon as the source of all heresy.

If we view the account of John in the light of the tradition several possibilities emerge. (1) The reference to the woman with whom Simon associated may explain the reason for the employment of the woman symbolism in the narrative. (2) The Simon Magus tradition clarifies the obscure statement of Jesus: "You are right in saying, 'I have no husband'; for you have had five husbands, and he whom you now have is not your husband." From this point of view the five husbands would be the five gods mentioned in 2 Kings 17:24 ff.; the consort of the woman would be Simon the magician, himself as spurious a god as those the Samaritans had worshiped of old. This would support the antimagical character of the Fourth Gospel.

The worship of Simon as a god would assume that salvation came from Samaria. This the Fourth Gospel refutes: "You worship what you do not know; we worship what we know, for salvation is out of the Jews." At the end the Samaritans recognize this for they affirm that this is indeed the Savior of the world.

Implications of this interpretation of the Samaritan woman story may be stated as follows: (1) It is correct methodology to look for sources of John within the New Testament itself and in the history of Christianity and related movements. (2) The mind of the Gospel writer is attracted to passages which contain an emphasis on the Holy Spirit. In this case his source contained the account of a perverted concept of the Spirit. This gives him an opportunity to correct it and is the same device used throughout the Gospel itself where Jesus "corrects" the lower meanings drawn from verbal symbols. (3) The book of Acts must be considered as a source for the Fourth Gospel. It would be strange indeed if this were not so, for the author of Acts has a profound interest in the concept of the Spirit. The Acts of the Apostles is actually "the acts of the Holy Spirit through the Apostles." (4) The way in which the evangelist uses his sources illustrates his creative literary ability. What is omitted from his sources, as well as what is included, makes possible a universalizing of the issues involved in the original statement. In this case, the Johannine account becomes a statement on the true nature of religion as contrasted with the false and so is relevant to any circumstance. The Gospel writer uses a source only to move away from it to a universal frame of reference. His selectivity and arrangement of material marks him as a literary genius and a man of refined religious sensitivity.

5. An adequate interpretation of the Gospel must take into account its dramatic character. The Gospel illustrates the dramatic technique of contrast: light and darkness; belief and unbelief; life and death. It abounds in dramatic scenes: The raising of Lazarus; the prediction by the high priest of Jesus' death; the anointing of Jesus; the voice from heaven; the demonstration of humility; the betrayal; Jesus before Pilate.

An excellent illustration of the dramatic technique of

John is embodied in the account of Jesus and Pilate (19:13). Macgregor recognizes this when he writes:

Undoubtedly the meaning is that Pilate set Jesus upon the tribunal, rather than that he took his own seat in order to pronounce final judgment in presence of the crowd. The story is so understood by Justin Martyr (*Apol.* I, 35), and in the *Gospel according to Peter*. This interpretation makes the scene much more dramatic and alone suits the words, "There is your king!" . . . Dramatically the Jews are shown rejecting their king. Pilate makes one final attempt to have the case laughed out of court; but John thinks not of the ridicule but of the unconscious prophecy: it is really Jesus who is King and Judge.[8]

The consummate art of the Gospel is recognized in these instances only as a reader is aware of the evangelist's concept of Jesus as divine Son of God. Here is God's revelation actually dwelling with men. And yet they are entirely oblivious to it. Not only are they oblivious to it, but they take the Divine One and crucify him. Here is the deep pathos of the human situation. The light was shining in the darkness and the darkness, like an active force, tried to extinguish it. But its apparent success in the crucifixion proved to be false, for the cross itself, in this Gospel, is no other than the gate of heaven, for by it Jesus is glorified. So the redemptive activity of God goes on and out of the gruesome fact of crucifixion

[8] G. H. C. Macgregor, *The Gospel of John* (New York: Harper & Brothers, 1928), p. 342. This passage also illustrates the Gospel writer's interest in Jesus' death as the time of his judgment on the world. See p. 169, n.

emerges the abiding presence of the life-giving Spirit in the little fellowship and eventually in the wider world beyond.

The methodology of the writer argues against the theory that there are radical dislocations of the text of the Fourth Gospel. The assumption that there are these dislocations has resulted in many attempts to rearrange the blocks of material in the "original" sequence. The best known and perhaps most radical rearrangement is found in Moffatt's translation of the New Testament.[9] For example, Moffatt transposes 3:22-30 between 2:12 and 2:13 with the explanation that this is its "true position."

Bultmann has added the weight of his great scholarship to the support of the transposers. He rearranges the content of the Gospel as follows:

1:1-3:36; 3:22-30; 4; 6:1-59; 5:1-47; 7:15-24; 8:13-20; 7:1-14, 25-52; 8:48-50, 54-55; 8:41-47, 51-53, 56-69; 9:1-41; 8:12; 12:44-50; 8:21-29; 12:34-36; 10:19-21; 10:22-26, 11-13, 1-10, 14-18, 27-39; 10:40-12:33; 8:30-40; 6:60-71; 12:27-43; 13:1-30; 13:1; 17:1-26; 13:31-35; 15:1-16:33; 13:36-14:31; 18:1-21:25.

His arguments rest in part upon his complicated theory of the literary origin of the Gospel, in part upon chance (the editor found some parts accidentally disarranged), but basically as do those of the other scholars upon certain precon-

[9] James Moffatt, *The New Testament, a New Translation* (New York: Harper & Brothers, 1922).

ceptions as to what was possible to the author of an early Christian gospel.[10] This last area is full of pitfalls, and leads here, we believe, to an unintended modernizing of the Gospel.

The case for radical dislocation of the text is based on a twofold argument:

1. The material at certain points is not in logical sequence. Consequently, Moffatt transposes 7:15-24 so as to follow 5:47, the point of connection being the Sabbath controversy with which both sections deal. Macgregor, commenting on this transposition says:

In their usual position these verses [7:15-24] are clearly out of place. They occur in the account of Jesus' visit to the Feast of Tabernacles in October. Yet without any explanation, particular reference is made to the effect produced by "one deed" performed at the Feast of Pentecost the previous May, since when Jesus has been absent from Galilee (7:1). The emphasis again on *one* miracle (7:21) seems inconsistent with the people's testimony to Jesus' *many* miracles (7:31). Finally, 7:20 ("Who wants to kill you?") seems incongruous if placed immediately before 7:25 ("Is this not the man they want to kill?"), though the latter verse is perfectly consistent with 7:1 ("the Jews were trying to kill him"). On the other hand, the thought of 7:15-24 is obviously a continuation of that of Chapter 5. Apart from the main topic, the violation of the Sabbath, note how 7:16-17 is an echo of 5:30-32, 7:18 of 5:41 ff., 7:19 of 5:45ff. The usual position of the section

[10] Bultmann, *op. cit.*, at the points where he abandons the canonical order.

may be due to a copyist, on the look-out for a suitable place to insert a fragment already displaced from its true position, having noticed the apparent connexion between Jesus' "teaching" in 7:14 and the Jews' "marvelling" at his letters in 7:15.[11]

An examination of this procedure reveals certain weaknesses. The argument that the reference to *one* miracle seems inconsistent fails to take into account the methodology of the evangelist who repeatedly resorts to cross-references. This method is made clear in 4:46 where the reference is to 2:1-11, but other examples are found in 5:33, a reference to 1:19 ff.; 7:50 which refers to 3:1; 10:31 which refers to Jesus' *many* signs as contrasted with *one* sign; 11:8 which refers to 10:31; 11:37 which refers to 9:1 ff.; 12:9 which refers to 11:1 ff.; 13:33, which refers to 7:33; 14:28 which refers to 14:2-3; 15:20 which refers to 13:16; 18:9 which refers to 17:12; 18:14 which refers to 11:49-50; 18:32 which refers to 3:14 and 12:32, 33; 19:7 which refers to 5:18 and 10:33; 19:39 which refers to 3:1; 20:21 which refers to 17:18 and 1:32-33. The reference in 7:21 must be placed in the same category. It merely refers to the miracle which had been detailed in the Gospel and which the author found valuable for the creation of a new teaching situation.

The fallacy in the appeal to logic is that the logic of the Gospel writer and that of the reader of the Gospel may not

[11] Macgregor, *op. cit.*, pp. 187-88.

coincide. Thorough acquaintance with the methodology employed by him leads to the conclusion that he was not interested in logical development at all.

2. Another reason for rearrangement, it is claimed, is that the discourse changes without notice from one character to another or from one character to the evangelist himself. Thus, it is suggested that 3:31-36, which as it stands contains the words of John the Baptist, should be attributed to Jesus and so calls for rearrangement. Moffatt places it after 3:21 and moves 3:22-30 to its "true" position between 2:12 and 2:13. Macgregor, on the other hand, thinks it should follow 3:13 where the contrasted ideas of "heaven" and "earth" are again resumed.[12]

Again, the methodology of the evangelist is the determining factor. In this Gospel incidents and comment upon the incidents merge imperceptibly into one another. The language of all the characters is identical. They all use the same vocabulary and they all talk about the same things. The vocabulary and selection of ideas are due to the author, and this means that the argument from shifts in language and ideas is valueless.

When this principle is applied to 3:31-36 it becomes evident that there is no real reason to change its position in the account. Quite the contrary, the entire section is a carrying

[12] *Ibid.*, p. 77.

forward of the witness of John to Jesus, for it was he who had seen the Spirit descend "without measure" upon Jesus. This is a reaffirmation, in more specific terms, of the nature of Jesus as spirit, already indicated by John in 1:29-34.

The argument advanced here does not rule out the possibility of some dislocations of the text. The clearest possibility of this is at the end of chapter fourteen, and the beginning of chapter fifteen.[13] The problem is one of transition from 14:31 to 15:1. Macgregor places chapter fourteen after 16:33, and it must be admitted that this aids the problem of transition.[14] In general, however, it remains true that rearrangement of the text must be undertaken with the greatest caution. The failure of some of our most distinguished scholars to reach agreement on the details of the rearrangement emphasizes the need for caution. There is no reason to think that such extensive changes were made as Moffatt's translation suggests, as Bultmann's commentary contains.

Having dealt with the areas of purpose and methodology we are now in a better position to examine the way in which the fourth evangelist viewed Jesus. This view, as we understand it, will be set forth in the next three chapters.

[13] The injunction to the disciples, "Rise, let us go hence," may be for the simple purpose of lending the illusion of movement to the account; a Gospel demands action.

[14] Macgregor, *op. cit.*, p. 285.

IV

The Divine Nature of Jesus

⚜⚜⚜⚜⚜⚜⚜⚜⚜

THROUGHOUT the Fourth Gospel Jesus is a divine being. It is true that he had a human body, but he was essentially divine. The Logos is the mechanism employed in the prologue of the Gospel to link Jesus with pre-existent deity. The Spirit performs the same function in the body of the Gospel. This same Jesus who was Logos before the world was created appears in this Gospel as the "God" of the Christians. No indication is given that he comes from the lower classes. He comes from a village, it is true, but the stage on which he plays his divine role is the city of Jerusalem. Galilee and the villages fade into the background of the gospel story. Instead of preaching tours through all the villages of Galilee, Jesus commutes between Galilee and Jerusalem.

The attention of the reader is focused sharply on Jerusalem in John not only by the location of a large number of incidents either in Jerusalem or en route to Jerusalem, but also by the weeding out of many casual references to Jesus and his followers as Galileans. This elimination of the provincial flavor can be clearly seen; e.g., in the story of Peter's denial. In Matthew 26:69-75, the first accusation against Peter is that he was "with Jesus of Galilee." The second time, he is accused of having been with Jesus the *Nazoraios*; and the third time, the accusers comment on his provincial dialect. In Mark 14:66-72, Peter is first accused of having been "with Jesus the Nazarene," then of being "one of them," and, third, of being "a Galilean," i.e., a Christian. In Luke 22:54-62, it is not till the third accusation that he is charged with being a Galilean: "Certainly this one was with him, too, for he also is a Galilean." But in the story of Peter's denial in the Fourth Gospel there is no association of either Jesus or Peter with Galilee. In 18:17 the maid asks, "Aren't you also one of the disciples of this man?" In 18:25 exactly the same question is repeated. Then in 18:26 the motive lost by the removal of Peter as a Galilean is replaced by the introduction of a relative of the man Peter wounded, who asks, "Didn't I see you with him in the garden?" But no one hints that Peter was an obvious provincial. This charge, which the first three evangelists quote as a just one against Peter, is in John brought against Nicodemus of Jerusalem without justification to show up in bright light the fanatical opposition of the Jews to Jesus (7:52).

In this Gospel Jesus has all the attributes of divinity. He

has supernatural knowledge, supernatural power and supernatural calm. He walks upon the stage in the first scene of this Gospel clad in the full panoply of divinity and moves majestically and irresistibly through the program on which he and his divine Father have agreed. Humility is alien to the glory of this divine being, as is compassion. The scene of the Good Shepherd in early Christian art derived nothing but the name from the Fourth Gospel. The Good Shepherd of Luke and Matthew is one who cannot rest while even one sheep out of a hundred is lost; he seeks diligently till he finds it, and carries it home on his shoulders. The Good Shepherd of John is the one true leader of the flock; he lays down his life for the flock to take it up again, and the laying down of his life as well as its resumption is due to the command of the Father. Nowhere in the Johannine account is there any sentiment of compassion.

Every action of Jesus in the Fourth Gospel is divinely motivated. Jesus works miracles of healing not because he sympathizes with the sick, but that he may manifest his glory. A man was born blind in order that Jesus by healing him might show himself to be the Light of the World. Jesus lets Lazarus die and stays away from the sisters for four days so that the resurrection may demonstrate that Jesus is the Resurrection and the Life. All Jesus' actions and all his words are manifestations of the divine glory which the Father bestowed upon him before Abraham's day.

It is due to this consistent presentation of Jesus as a divine and glorious being that the fourth evangelist omits the emphasis upon the astonishment with which Jesus' mighty works are received by the crowds in the earlier gospels. In these earlier gospels—especially in Mark—almost every miracle of Jesus is received with astonishment or fear (e.g., Mark 2:12; 4:40; 5:15; 5:42). In these stories Jesus is not such a one as would be expected to perform truly supernatural acts; but in John the manifestation of his divine power does not astonish people. It is true that the disciples "marvel" at his talking with a woman (4:27); the Jews marvel at his teaching because they know he had no schooling (7:15); and Jesus asserts that the Jews all marvel because he did one work (7:21). This last sounds like an echo of earlier tradition and cannot be paralleled in John in the record of the crowd's reaction to Jesus' mighty works. In this Gospel, the usual result of Jesus' miracles is not astonishment or fear, but belief in Jesus (2:11; 6:14; 9:38; 11:45).

Humility is not a characteristic of Jesus in this Gospel. Not here can he say, I am meek and lowly. What he says in the scenes of this Gospel are the words he heard in heaven; all the words of Jesus in John are proud words. The Jesus of John is slapped on one cheek, but there is not humiliation in the retort with which he rebukes the smiter. John and Matthew are the only Gospels that quote Zechariah 9:9 in the triumphal entry, but John differs from Zechariah and Matthew in that he omits the word "lowly." Not abasement but exaltation is the keynote of Jesus' teaching. In the Synoptics he teaches his followers that the Son of man must suffer many things; in John, that he must be exalted.

There is one scene in John in which humility is at least the "bodily" meaning, but it is a lesson for disciples—not a revelation of Jesus' nature. Jesus washed his disciples' feet as an example to them of what they should do, but not because they were tired and he felt sorry for them. He seems to step out of character for a moment and puts on this demonstration for the benefit of his disciples. When he is through he calls their attention to his condescension. This puzzling pericope, introduced here as a substitute for the institution of the Lord's Supper, was probably intended to have some "spiritual" (i.e., symbolical) meaning.

Bultmann convincingly suggests[1] that this act symbolizes the disciples' acceptance of the service Jesus renders man. This service is not the physical act, the foot washing, an act of loving-kindness, but the revelation of God. Peter's objection is understandable from this point of view. If Jesus were acting out of compassion, Peter would accept it. But what he

[1] Bultmann, *op. cit.*, pp. 356 f.

finds hard to accept is "service" from the divine Jesus—to be a disciple of one who will be glorified by a cross. This may approach humility through insistence on revelation through this specific individual, but it did not include the message that Jesus was humble in the sense carried by the earlier gospels. Not the Jesus who says, "You call me Teacher and Lord, and you say well; for so I am."

As a consequence of Jesus' foreknowledge and his complete control of all situations, there is in John no sense of stress, none of the elements of tragedy so familiar in the earlier gospels. The Jesus of John is too much one with God for a Gethsemane to be possible. For him there can be no sorrow or defeat in a betrayal, since that was part of God's plan and Jesus had actually chosen Judas to betray him. In the Fourth Gospel the divine Jesus whom Paul knew only after the resurrection appears on every page and in every scene. The evangelist intends his reader to follow the words and deeds of this divine Jesus to a faith like that of Thomas, who hails him as "My Lord and my God!" But there is no contrast in quality here between the earthly and the risen Lord; they are equally divine, and equally of cosmic significance.

To the cultured pagan the story of Gethsemane seemed to lack the dignity that was one of the attributes of deity. The withdrawal to the garden at night resembled an attempt at flight.[2] The saying about swords suggested that a god might need to depend on the arms of his followers for defense. Jesus' fervent prayer for deliverance from his fate seemed strange on the lips of a divine being. Celsus leaps to attack the Gethsemane prayer: "Why does he mourn, and lament, and pray to escape the fear of death, expressing himself in terms like these—'O Father, if it be possible, let this cup pass from me'?"[3] Origen's answer is that the inclusion of such details is an indication of the evangelists' love of truth, for otherwise they would certainly have omitted incidents that were so unattractive. By advancing such a defense Origen reveals his own awareness of the difficulties caused by the Synoptic Passion story.

In the Gospel of Nicodemus the unsuitability of the Gethsemane scene in the life of a god is dramatically indicated. Reports of Jesus' approach have reached the underworld. Satan is reassuring Hades, who has been greatly impressed by a summary of Jesus' mighty deeds. "But I know that he is a man," says Satan, "For I heard him say 'My soul is exceedingly sorrowful unto death.'" To this Hades replies with a warning, "But if you say that you heard him fearing death, he said this to mock and deceive you so that he might capture you the more securely."[4] Origen says plainly with ref-

[2] Origen, *Celsus*, ii.9.

[3] *Ibid.*, ii.24; see also vii.55.

[4] Gospel of Nicodemus xxI f., in C. Tischendorf, *Evangelia apocrypha* (2nd ed., Leipzig, 1876), pp. 326-27.

erence to this saying in Gethsemane that not even the Christians claim that this is the divine Jesus; these sayings spring from the human nature of the Savior. He is not a god when he says, "My soul is exceedingly sorrowful unto death."[5]

But John's answer is quite different from this. For him, the first three Gospels are not sacred and authoritative books which must be defended. He, therefore, takes all but a trace of Gethsemane out of the story. This vestige of Gethsemane is not generally recognized, since John has transferred it to a place immediately before the last meal (12:27-30). Jesus is momentarily troubled in his heart as he announces that the time for his death has come. "What," he says, "shall I say? Shall I pray 'Father, save me from this trial!' [As Matthew, Mark and Luke report.] No, that would be nonsense, since I came into the world for the specific purpose of dying this way. Therefore, I will ask the Father to glorify his name by my exaltation upon the cross as a final manifestation of his glory."

This is a direct repudiation of the earlier Gethsemane prayer, which was an impossible prayer for the impassive Messenger of this Gospel. In its place, we find a characteristic Johannine prayer, which turns out not to be a prayer at all. That is to say, Jesus does not make the request for himself,

[5] *Celsus* ii.9, with reference to Mark 14:34 (equals Matt. 26:38).

but for others who stand by. When the voice from heaven comes, Jesus carefully informs the bystanders that it comes on their account, not on his. He does not take a single step away from the destiny which he himself helped to set. This explanation of the significance of the prayer is what forces John to locate his Gethsemane story before the Last Supper. A prayer in the interest of unbelievers must be delivered when unbelievers are present to receive the answer; therefore this prayer must be a part of the public ministry of Jesus before he and his withdraw to the upper room.[6] The voice from heaven is the last great sign of Jesus' public ministry.

An interesting detail of the Johannine Gethsemane is the comment of the crowd on the voice. Some displayed the gross misunderstanding which characterizes all the audiences of this Gospel, and heard nothing but thunder. But others claimed that it was an angel speaking to him. There is much to recommend the suggestion of Goguel that this shows knowledge of the story about the bloody sweat and the ministering angel which we find in some manuscripts in Luke 22:43-44.[7] But even those who regarded the voice as angelic were, of course, wrong. It was the Father who spoke. No angels come between Jesus and God in this book, nor

[6] See Maurice Goguel, *Les sources du récit Johannique de la Passion* (Paris, 1910), p. 49; and W. Bauer, *Das Johannesevangelium* (3rd ed., Tuebingen, 1933) on 12:27.

[7] Goguel, *op. cit.*, p. 48, n. 3.

(79)

does Jesus have any weakness or sense of separation from God which would require angelic ministration.

In John, Jesus goes into a garden to be arrested, not to strive with God in prayer. There is only a trace of the suffering which is the main motif of the earlier stories. In the scene described in the twelfth chapter of John, it is the bystanders who experience Gethsemane, not Jesus.

One faint echo of the earlier Gethsemane story survives in John's account of the cutting off of Malchus' ear. In Mark there is no comment on this; in Luke it is the occasion for a miracle; in Matthew there is more consciousness of the ludicrous futility of that blow—the disciple is rebuked by the quotation of a proverb, by a reference to the angelic host who could defend Jesus, and by an appeal to the necessary fulfillment of Scripture. In John, Peter strikes the blow and is rebuked by Jesus for suggesting by such an action that Jesus was not ready to drink the cup which his Father had offered him (18:10-11).[8] The reference to the legion of angels is replaced by a demonstration of Jesus' (supernatural) power to defend himself (18:4-6). But this is only a demonstration of power, not a serious attempt to use it. It was one of Jesus'

[8] This serves the function also of Jesus' rebuke of Peter for his suggestion that Jesus should not die, after the confession in Mark 8:29 f. In John both the Messiahship and the crucifixion have been announced long before this point; so the confession becomes a declaration of the unique value of Jesus' teaching, and Judas (not Peter) is identified with Satan.

followers, not Jesus himself, who revolted at the thought of the imminent catastrophe.

For Jesus is here portrayed as calmly and confidently following a program which he had accepted in its entirety long before. He sees the end from the beginning, sees it clearly and sees it constantly. He predicted his death in his first public action at Jerusalem (2:19-21). He explained the necessity of his death to Nicodemus (3:14). The "hour" of his death was fixed before the ministry began, and both Jesus and the evangelist were constantly aware of it. In such a situation the earlier Gethsemane incident could serve no useful function. The Johannine repudiation of it was almost inevitable.

Even more shocking to respectable people was the story that the divine Lord of the Christians had been betrayed by one of his chosen intimates. This was part of the gospel Paul had received and passed on to the Corinthians.[9] But the betrayal caused no difficulty in Paul's thinking, since for him the earthly life of Jesus was a life of humiliation, emptied of divinity. For him the manifestation of Jesus' glory was the resurrection; he did not search back of it for any indication of Jesus' divine nature; on the contrary, he looked further ahead to the second coming for the full revelation of the glory of the heavenly Jesus. But the resurrection appear-

[9] I Cor. 11:23.

ances ceased, and the hope of the second coming was not fulfilled. Devout Christians began to look back to Jesus' life on earth for evidences of his divine attributes. His divinity is an open secret in Mark, the glory being reflected onto the events of his ministry from the resurrection which has not yet taken place, on one occasion breaking out to dazzle his most intimate disciples. In the second century this tendency reaches completion, and the earthly life of Jesus is claimed for the God-Jesus.

It is the Christians' claim that Jesus of Galilee fully revealed his divinity on earth that makes a problem of the betrayal. Celsus' statement on the betrayal is a clear presentation of the difficulty:

. . . he who was a god could neither flee nor be led away a prisoner; and least of all could he be deserted and delivered up by those who had been his associates, and had shared all things in common, and had had him for their teacher, who was deemed to be a savior, and a son of the greatest god, and an angel.[10]

It was incredible to the thinking pagan that a divine Jesus could have been betrayed.

It was equally incredible to John. The betrayal in the Fourth Gospel is purely a matter of form. It was planned by God before the incarnation. Jesus chose Judas to play the part of the betrayer. "For Jesus knew from the first who would not believe and who was going to betray him" (6:64).

[10] *Celsus* ii.9; see also ii.12.

Jesus of course carries out the Father's will in this respect, and so do the disciples! The most striking example of the lack of human values in the relation of Jesus to his disciples in this Gospel is shown in their acquiescence in his betrayal. He tells them after the feeding of the five thousand that one of them is a devil (i.e., as the evangelist explains, a traitor). This announcement is repeated at the Last Supper, and the traitor is pointed out to Peter and the disciple whom Jesus especially loved (13:21-28). The disciples do nothing to prevent the betrayal. To interfere would have been to go against both Jesus and his Father.[11] Jesus himself tells Judas to proceed with the betrayal (13:27-30). This may seem incredible in the story of a man and his friends, but it is very plausible in the relations of a divine being with those mortals whom he has chosen. It is part of the elevation of the betrayal to cosmic significance that we note in the omission of the price paid to Judas. Judas made no bargain with Jesus' enemies; nothing so mundane as a handful of silver motivates the betrayal. Judas acted in accordance with the divine plan.[12] Every criticism of Jesus as a God that was raised by the

[11] The references to Satan as suggesting the betrayal at most supply only a secondary cause, and may be the preservation of an earlier attempt to solve the problem. See Luke 22:3-6. John's agreements with Luke are especially numerous in the Passion narrative; see list of parallels in Vincent Taylor, *Formation of the Gospel Tradition* (London, 1933), p. 53, n. 1.

[12] This is the more striking in that John has portrayed Judas as a covetous thief in 12:4-6. His protest over the money wasted, a protest arising from his desire to get the money for himself, may be the Johannine substitute for the story of the thirty pieces of silver.

(83)

earlier betrayal stories is answered by the Johannine narrative of the betrayal.

One of the best known features of the Judas story is omitted by John to answer criticisms of the arrest of Jesus: Judas does not betray Jesus with a kiss. This is because John, like the cultured critics of Christianity in the second century, could not conceive of a god as arrested and forcibly carried off to stand trial. In the earlier gospels, the kiss of Judas was a signal by which Judas identified Jesus so that the posse might seize him and hurry him away. But in John, when the appointed hour comes Jesus identifies himself and allows the military to carry him off for trial. But not before the hour agreed on by God and Jesus. Before that moment, attempts to arrest him are numerous but vain (7:30, 32, 44-46; 8:20; 10:39). Nor is Jesus surprised and overpowered. He tells his followers before they enter the garden that the arresting party will soon arrive (14:30-31). When they approach, Jesus goes out to meet them in full knowledge of what they are planning to do. He takes charge of his own arrest, as a god should. He asks them whom they are looking for, states his identity, and manifests that divine power which in Matthew is merely mentioned. He who can knock a detachment of troops to the ground with a word has no need of legions of angels. But this exercise of divine power was not intended as an attempt at defense; it merely proved that Jesus had the power to defend himself and was not, there-

THE DIVINE NATURE OF JESUS

fore, overpowered. The disciples who in earlier accounts took to their heels are here dismissed with dignity after Jesus has secured immunity for them from the authorities. This happened to fulfill his own prediction (18:8-9; cf. also 17:12). The whole story of the arrest has become the story of a divine being acting as divinity should act in what otherwise might be an awkward or trying situation.

To be arrested is disgrace enough, but to be condemned is worse. "Christus, the founder of the sect, was put to death as a criminal by the procurator Pontius Pilate, in the reign of Tiberius."[13] The enemies of Christianity were not slow to see that the condemnation of Jesus by Pilate was a weapon fitted to their hands. In a society dominated by Rome the condemnation of Jesus by a Roman official severely discredited his cult. An oracle of Apollo (quoted by Porphyry) refers to the God of a Christian woman as "her God whom just judges condemned to an evil death."[14] If Jesus, who was sentenced by Pilate, was the Son of God, why was Pilate never punished by God for his crime?[15] The verdict of Pilate proved that Jesus was a criminal; otherwise he would have been acquitted. From the verdict of "guilty" at Jesus' trial arose the accusation that Jesus was a sinner.[16]

The main line of Christian defense of Jesus from the

[13] Tacitus, *Annals* xv.44.
[14] Friedlaender, *Roman Life and Manners under the Early Empire* (London and New York, 1908), I, 259.
[15] Origen, *Celsus* ii.34 f.; viii.39, 41.
[16] Origen, *Celsus* ii.41.

charge of being a condemned criminal was to place the responsibility on the Jews and make Pilate a Christian champion.[17] If a Roman official did not condemn Jesus, the charge lost much of its power; if the sentence were due to the enmity of the despised Jews, it would attract Gentiles to Jesus instead of repelling them. This shifting of the responsibility for the verdict against Jesus from Pilate, where it rightfully belonged, to the Jews, began in the first generation of Christian history. From Paul to Chrysostom, and after, the Jews are blamed for the death of Jesus.

Paul characterizes the Jews as those "who killed the Lord Jesus, and persecuted the prophets and us."[18] In Matthew, Pilate openly said: "I am not responsible for this man's death; you must see to it yourselves." And the Jews answered, "His blood be on us and on our children."[19] In Luke-Acts, Pilate three times declared Jesus innocent, as Herod did once; and Stephen, Peter and Paul exonerate Pilate and put the blame on the Jews.[20] Barnabas,[21] the Preaching of Peter,[22] Aristides,[23] Justin Martyr,[24] and Ter-

---

[17] For a discussion of this change see C. H. Moehlman, *The Christian-Jewish Tragedy* (Rochester and New York, 1933), chap. 3, "The Christian Reinterpretation of Pilate."

[18] I Thess. 2:15.

[19] Matt. 27:24-25.

[20] Luke 23:4, 14-16, 21-22. Acts 7:52; 2:36; 3:13-14; 4:10; 13:27-29.

[21] *Epistle of Barnabas* vii.9.

[22] English translation in M. R. James, *The Apocryphal New Testament*, p. 18.

[23] *Apology* xv.2.

[24] *I Apology* lxiii.10, 16; *Dialogue* xviii.1, lxxxv.2.

tullian,[25] speak for the Christians as a whole when they say, "Jesus was slain by the Jews in the time of Pontius Pilate." Pilate's significance is reduced to that of a date line; the Jews are the judges and executioners. Pilate is not punished for the death of Jesus because he was not responsible for it; the Jews were responsible and they were punished in the years A. D. 70 and 135 by crushing defeat in war and the loss of temple and homeland.[26]

John's account of the trial of Jesus fits harmoniously into the defense made by other Christians in the first two centuries. Bauer claims that John's presentation of the trial is ruled throughout by the apologetic interest.[27] His story agrees with Luke's very closely, for Luke was as anxious as John to clear the Roman government of responsibility for Jesus' death. Pilate three times declared to the Jews that he found Jesus innocent (18:39; 19:4, 6); he tried to satisfy the Jews by having Jesus flogged (19:1-5); when he found out that the charge against Jesus was that he claimed to be the Son of God, he quizzed Jesus, was convinced of his divine nature and tried to find a way to let him go (19:7-12). But the bitter and unflagging hostility of the Jews finally forced Pilate to turn Jesus over to them to be crucified.

In the trial, as at the arrest, Jesus is more powerful than

[25] *Apology* xxi.18.
[26] Origen, *Celsus* ii.34.
[27] *Johannesevangelium* (3rd ed.), p. 221.

his enemies, but he acquiesces in their actions because he knows that what they are doing is in accord with the divine plan. He tells Pilate plainly, "You would have no power at all over me if it were not given to you from above" (19:11). Pilate could not avoid crucifying Jesus (however much he might want to) because the divine Jesus had predicted his own death by crucifixion, and the words of a deity must be fulfilled (18:32). In John, the trial of Jesus is the trial of a god. The only disturbance of its dignity is the mistreatment of Jesus by the Jews before the High Priest (18:19-23).[28] Even this is turned by Jesus into a demonstration of his innocence, since the Jews are unable to justify the mistreatment.

But the most repellent feature of the Passion story was the manner of Jesus' death. The divine Savior of the Christians was executed as the lowest criminals were executed. Crucifixion was a method of execution reserved for traitors, pirates, perjurers, rebels, murderers, slaves, etc., who were not Roman citizens; yet the Lord of the Christian cult was crucified. No other divine being was so disgraced. Justin is aware of parallels between many details of the Christian gospel about Jesus and contemporary pagan myths. These parallels, he feels, are due to the plan of the demons to dis-

[28] There are striking resemblances between this passage and the account of Paul before the High Priest in Acts 23:1-5.

credit Christianity by using the material supplied by the prophets (!) to set up similar stories that would detract from the uniqueness of the Christian gospel. He is somewhat puzzled by their failure to parallel the crucifixion.[29] There was no parallel claimed for pagan gods because of the liability that would be assumed with the cross. In the nineteenth century the hangman's noose would not commend itself to many as a religious symbol.

Ridicule and disdain met the story of the crucified God in Palestine and in the Gentile world, especially from the members of the better classes. Paul's evidence on this point cannot be overemphasized.[30] From Paul to Eusebius, the pages of early Christian literature testify to the strength of the opposition to the message of the cross. The opponents of Christianity not only point out that Jesus died by "a most miserable death,"[31] but also insist that this must have been due to his lack of ability to help himself.[32] This charge is brought forward in direct connection with the crucifixion in our first three Gospels.

And the passers-by jeered at him, shaking their heads and saying, "Aha! you who would tear down the sanctuary and build

---

[29] Justin explains the demons' omission as due to their failure to understand the symbolism of the prophecies. *I Apology* xxii.4; xxiii.3; liv.4; lv.1; *Dialogue* lxix.

[30] Note the appeal to common recognition of the fact that the cross was an obstacle, Gal. 5:11.

[31] Origen, *Celsus* vii.53.

[32] "Even if he was crucified through weakness," 2 Cor. 13:4.

one in three days! Come down from the cross and save yourself!"
The high priests too made sport of him to one another with the
scribes and said, "He saved others, but he cannot save himself!
Let this Christ, the king of Israel, come down from the cross
now, so that we may see it and believe!" And the men who were
crucified with him abused him.[33]

Christian apologists had to face the question, "Why couldn't
Christ help himself?"[34] The problem that was inherent in
the story of a slain god is raised for pagan cults by Aristides
the Christian. He attacks the self-sufficiency of Isis, Aphro-
dite, Dionysus, Hercules, and others, as gods who suffered
or were slain. His indictment of each is, "He was not able
to help himself; how shall he help others?"[35] It is a strange
commentary on the blindness of faith that Aristides is one
of the very few defenders of Christianity who does not meet
this charge as made against Jesus himself. Nor does this
early apologist mention the trial or the crucifixion in his
outline of Jesus' career.

But pagan ridicule of the crucifixion was not limited to
literary forms of expression. The mimes, the burlesque show
of the Roman world, often used kings and deities as subjects
for their ridicule.[36] When King Agrippa I visited Alex-

[33] Mark 15:29-32. See Matt. 27:39-44; Luke 23:35-39.

[34] Origen, *Celsus* i.54.

[35] E.g., *Apology* x.8; xi.3; x.9; xii.2-9.

[36] Hermann Reich, *Der Mimus* (Berlin, 1902); and "Der Mann mit dem
Eselskopf. Ein Mimodrama, vom klassischen Altertum verfolgt bis auf Shake-
speare," *Jahrbuch der deutschen Shakespeare-gesellschaft* XL (1904), p. 116.

THE DIVINE NATURE OF JESUS

andria in A.D. 38, the anti-Semitists made a public mockery
of him. A naked fool was given a throne in the gymnasium,
a diadem of paper, a doormat as a robe and a papyrus stalk
as a scepter. He was also given a bodyguard and was hailed
with mock reverence as a king. This was done, says Philo,
in imitation of theatrical usage in the mimes.[37] Tertullian
refers to the ridicule of Anubis, Diana, Jove and Hercules
in the mimes.[38] Some of the figures in the mimes were given
animal heads. Aeneas, Anchises and Ascanius appear with
dog heads in a scene from the mimes on the walls of Pom-
peii;[39] the speaking ass or man with an ass's head appears as
early as the first century, A.D.[40] It is therefore highly probable
that the famous Palatine sketch may be a third-century attempt to picture a scene from the mimes. In it we see a
figure with an ass's head on the cross, with a man standing
before it in adoration, and the inscription "Alexamenos
worships his God."[41] Reich in his discussion of the mime of
the man with the ass's head asserts that in this Alexamenos
scene the figure on the cross is Jesus. He refers to the preva-
lence of crucifixion and baptism scenes in the mimes of the

[37] *Against Flaccus* v-vi.
[38] *Apology* xv.i. For bibliography, see Martin Schanz and Carl Hosius,
Geschichte der römischen Literatur (4th ed., *Handbuch der Altertums-wissenschaft*
VIII.i), Teil I (München, 1927), 254-55.
[39] Reich, *op. cit.*, p. 124.
[40] A scene from a first-century vase is reproduced by Reich, *ibid.*, p. 110.
[41] Reproduced in C. M. Kaufmann, *Handbuch der altchristlichen Epigraphik*
(Freiburg im Breisgau, 1917), p. 302.

first three centuries, and feels that this identification of the crucified man with an ass's head as Jesus is made the more certain by the syncretism of certain Christian sects which had been influenced by the cult of the ass-headed Seth.[42] Thus the ridicule of the Passion story found expression in the lower levels of drama and art as well as in literature.

Dramatic evidence of the Christians' sensitiveness to these objections to the Passion story can be seen in early Christian art. For the early Christians never represented the episodes of the Passion except in a veiled or symbolical manner. The cross itself appears in the catacombs only about twenty times before the fourth century, when it was no longer used as an instrument for the execution of criminals. Many of these early crosses are half disguised; e.g., in the form of the letter Tau (T), or as an anchor.[43] The earliest portrayals of the crucifixion present the cross more by suggestion than by fidelity to detail. This is true of three gems from the second and third centuries,[44] as also of the fifth-century monuments.[45] In only one of these cases is the cross plainly de-

[42] Reich, *op. cit.*, p. 124. See also the charge that the Christians worship an ass in Minucius Felix, *Octavius* ix.4.

[43] See the reproductions in Cabrol, *Dictionnaire d'archéologie chrétienne et de liturgie* (Paris, 1907), Vol. III, Pt. II, cols. 3053-54.

[44] Reproductions in Cabrol, *ibid.*, cols. 3049-50.

[45] A relief on the wooden door of S. Sabina in Rome, and an ivory relief in the British museum. Reproductions of both in Kaufmann, *Handbuch der christlichen Archaeologie* (3rd ed., Paderborn, 1922), pp. 358-59, Figs. 173-74. See also pp. 334 f., and O. M. Dalton, *A Guide to the Early Christian and Byzantine Antiquities in the Department of British and Medieval Antiquities* (2nd ed., British Museum, 1921), p. 88 and Pl. II (ivory).

picted; and, in most of them, the triumphant air of the crucified is further disguise. Christians may have used the crucifixion in private devotions, such as those ridiculed by the famous graffito of Alexamenos worshiping his god; but they were careful not to portray such scenes for the public to observe.[46] For public observation meant public ridicule.

Christian defense of the crucifixion developed along two lines. First, Jesus chose to die in accordance with God's will, not pagan compulsion; second, the association of the crucifixion with the resurrection in a close and vital relationship cast a glory even over the cross. Paul says that he inherited from earlier Christians the explanation that Jesus died for *our* sins (i.e., not his own) according to the Scriptures (i.e., God's plan, not Rome's decision).[47] For Paul it is the ultimate proof of Jesus' obedience to God's will that he should agree to the accursed death of the cross. This is a logical conclusion to the earthly career of Jesus as one emptied of divinity. In reward, Jesus is raised from the dead and restored to his glory as a divine being.[48] That Paul welds death and resurrection into an inseparable unit, God's plan of salvation, can be seen from a careful study of his letters.

In the Synoptic Gospels we find the same answers. Jesus died in fulfillment of Scripture, although it may be signifi-

[46] O. Marucchi, *Eléments d'archéologie chrétienne* (Paris and Rome, 1899), I, 312-13.
[47] 1 Cor. 15:3.
[48] Phil. 2:6-11.

cant that it is usually after the resurrection that the disciples'
minds are opened to the understanding of the predictions.[49]
Matthew is careful to point out that Jesus could have defended himself by the use of the angelic host if he had not
been willing to die. But he felt under compulsion to be
crucified so the Scripture might be fulfilled.[50] Each of the
evangelists is careful to emphasize that Jesus was fully aware
of his approaching death and resurrection. The rebuke of
Peter as Satan is caused by Peter's shrinking from the announcement of the approaching Passion. And in the sequel,
those who are ashamed of Jesus (an allusion to the crucifixion) are warned that at the second coming Jesus will be
ashamed of them.[51]

In the first half of the second century Polycarp gives a
summary of the doctrines of the false brothers who deceive
vain men:

For every one who does not acknowledge that Jesus Christ
came in flesh is Antichrist, and whoever does not acknowledge
the witness of the cross is of the devil, and whoever edits the
sayings of the Lord according to his own desires and says that
there is no resurrection or judgment is the eldest son of Satan.[52]

This is evidence that some Christians were trying to meet
the objection to incarnation, crucifixion, resurrection and

[49] E.g., Luke 24:45-47.
[50] Matt. 26:52-54.
[51] Mark 8:31-9:1.
[52] *To the Philippians* vii.1.

judgment by denying these four doctrines. The development of this heresy was the direct result of an attempt to conform the gospel to the interests and prejudices of the pagan world. Ignatius and the First Letter of John are further witnesses to this stress, as also to more orthodox attempts to meet objections.[53]

In the *Dialogue* of Justin Martyr, his Jewish opponent says: "This your so-called Christ is without honor and glory, so that he has even fallen into the uttermost curse that is in the Law of God, for He was crucified."[54] But Justin makes the old defense: ". . . why do you speak of him as an accursed person who agreed to suffer these things according to the will of his father?"[55] Predictions of the crucifixion crowd the pages of Justin's Old Testament.[56]

Origen meets the same attack from Celsus with the same replies. The Jew (in Celsus) says, "When we [Christians] declare the Logos to be the Son of God, we do not present to view a pure and holy Logos, but a most degraded man, who was punished by crucifixion."[57] But, says Origen, Jesus was great enough to overcome even "that apparently infamous death of crucifixion."[58] For the crucifixion was a voluntary

[53] Ignatius, *To the Philadelphians* viii.2: *Ephesians* xviii.
[54] *Dialogue* xxxii.1.
[55] *Ibid.*, xcv.2.
[56] *Ibid.*, lxxxvi-cv. Cf. *Barnabas* xi.8-xii.7.
[57] *Celsus* ii.31.
[58] *Celsus* i.30.

act on Jesus' part designed to serve humanity by overcoming the supreme evil spirit.[59] "And since . . . Celsus reproaches the Savior because of his sufferings, saying that he received no assistance from the Father, or was unable to aid himself; we have to state that his sufferings were the subject of prophecy, along with the cause of them. . . ."[60]

John's defense of the crucifixion agrees in general with that of other defenders. The distinctive features of his defense may be established by a contrasting of his treatment of crucifixion and resurrection with Paul's and his argument from prophecy with that in the Synoptics. For Paul the crucifixion is the last humiliating incident of the human life which Jesus lived in obedience to the Father's plan. This obedience was in no sense forced, though it involved a temporary abandonment of divinity. The crucifixion is a necessary prelude to the resurrection by which Jesus was shown to be the divine Messiah.

But in John, Jesus is the divine Messiah on earth as well as after the resurrection. The resurrection is merely the beginning of the return to the Father. And the glory shines on the crucifixion not from the resurrection which is to follow it, but from the life of divine revelation which has preceded it. As Bultmann phrases it, "The Departure is one

[59] *Celsus* i.31.
[60] *Celsus* i.54.

with the Coming." Jesus is such a glorious figure throughout this Gospel, so palpably divine, that for him to be crucified is to define crucifixion as part of a divine plan. This
conception of the earthly life of Jesus as a full manifestation of deity made it inevitable that the Johannine word for
crucifixion should be "exaltation."[61] This term combines in
one image the ascension of Jesus and his crucifixion. It is
used in Acts 2:33 and 5:31 of the ascension of Jesus, and John
uses it of the lifting up of Jesus on the cross, with a play on
words that is characteristic of his style. The important point
is, of course, the ascension of Jesus; but the point of departure is the elevation of the cross. That the loathsome
spectacle of an actual crucifixion should have suggested the
concept seems incredible.[62] It is more probable that the idea
was in part suggested by Scriptural "predictions" of the
Passion and from Luke's use of the word in Acts. Our author
found in the story of the lifting up of the brass serpent in
the wilderness a satisfying symbol of the crucifixion. Jesus'
application of this prediction to his own death (an application made from the beginning of his ministry) is later referred to as making death by crucifixion necessary.[63]

There is a minor but striking difference between Jesus'

[61] John 3:14; 8:28; 12:32 f.
[62] See W. Wrede, *Charakter und Tendenz des Johannesevangeliums* (Tuebingen and Leipzig, 1903), pp. 23 f; W. Heitmueller in *Die Schriften des Neuen
Testamentes* (2nd ed., Göttingen, 1907), II, 745 (or 3rd ed., IV, 68).
[63] John 18:32.

predictions of the Passion in the Synoptics and his predictions in John. In the Synoptics, Jesus warns his disciples of his approaching betrayal, mistreatment and death. "The Son of man will be handed over to the high priests and scribes and they will condemn him to death and hand him over to the heathen and they will ridicule him and spit on him and flog him and kill him; and after three days he will rise again."[64] Even before this he has notified his followers that he must suffer many things.[65] This somber and apprehensive note is entirely absent in John. Nowhere does Jesus announce any approaching suffering on his part. The betrayal is not predicted by Jesus till the last meal; in 6:71 and 12:4 as in 18:2, 5, "the one who was to betray Jesus" is a label to identify Judas. Nowhere does Jesus predict that others will kill him. Here the entire tone of these predictions is changed. Jesus is to be exalted; he is to return to his Father; he is now to have the glory that he had with the Father before the world was. His death is a planned departure full of benefits for all; the cross is his pathway to glory.

This glorification of the cross through interpreting it as the ladder by which Jesus ascends to the Father makes the ascension story of Luke-Acts an impossibility for John. There is, therefore, no ascension in John as a definite incident—

[64] Mark 10:32-34; Matt. 20:17-19; Luke 18:31-34; Matt. 17:22-23; Luke 9:43-45.
[65] Mark 8:31; 9:12.

aside from the crucifixion. Bauer says, "These two are for John inseparable." In 13:20-36 "to be lifted up" is used explicitly in the double sense of death by crucifixion and of Jesus' departure to the Father. Jesus announces that he must be lifted up. Thus, says the evangelist, he indicated the manner of his death. But the crowd protests that the Messiah was to stay with his people forever. "To be lifted up" was "to be lifted up to God." But in order that his followers may have an "abiding" Counselor, Jesus delays the consummation of the ascension until he has seen his followers and given them the Holy Spirit. But he is actually on his way to the Father when he sees Mary in the garden (20:17). Thus in John the crucifixion and the resurrection appearances are successive stages in one continuous process which is the ascension. But if John were forced to identify the ascension with one incident, he would mention the crucifixion. The refrain of the "farewell discourses" in 13-17 is "I am going now to the Father" (e.g., 17:13); the interval of forty days in Luke-Acts cannot be inserted in the unified, continuous Johannine ascension. One week's delay that the Spirit may be given, one week for the sake of Thomas; and the divine Jesus who was "hastening to heaven"[66] from the moment of the cross has returned to the Father.

[66] Cf. the divine assistant in K. Preisendanz, *P. Gr. Mag. I* (Leipzig and Berlin, 1928). After he has performed the tasks assigned to him by the one who knows the magical charms, he will say: "What else do you want? for I am hastening to heaven." Goodspeed and Colwell, *A Greek Papyrus Reader* (Chicago, 1935), p. 79, line 184.

In John, Jesus is fully aware of his approaching death, and the reader of the Gospel is constantly reminded of his knowledge. He is hailed by John the Baptist in terms that suggest sacrifice, and he predicts his death from the beginning of his ministry. The terms in which he explains the voluntary nature of his death go far beyond anything in the Synoptics. The allegory of the Good Shepherd is introduced to teach that Jesus died of his own free will. "This is why the Father loves me, because I am giving my life, but giving it to take it back again. No one has taken it from me, but I am giving it of my own accord. I have power to give it, and I have power to take it back again. These are the orders I have received from my Father" (10:17-18). As Jesus approached his death, he was "fully aware that the Father had put everything into his hands, and that he had come from God and was going back to God."[67]

He prepares his disciples for his approaching departure by announcing that he will send them a Counselor, the Spirit of Truth. In the "farewell discourses" Jesus explains his death as a necessary prelude to the coming of the Spirit. These parting remarks to the disciples, a distinctive Johannine feature, carry in every line evidence of Jesus' awareness of his approaching departure. For so dignified has his death become that it can be spoken of as a departure, a return to

[67] John 13:3.

the Father. And every incident is interpreted as part of the divine plan.

It is in this connection that the Old Testament is used by John. Almost every event of the Passion occurs to fulfill Scripture; while there are not more than six or seven allusions to the Old Testament elsewhere in John.[68] Moses and the serpent set the type for the death of Jesus (3:14); the Messiah enters on an ass's colt (12:14-16); the disbelief of the Jews was predicted by Isaiah (12:37-41; 15:25); the betrayal by a disciple was foretold (13:18; 17:12); the escape of the disciples and the execution by the Romans were predicted by Jesus himself (19:9, 32); the division of Jesus' clothes was controlled by Scripture (19:23-24); so also what he said from the cross (19:28), and the fact that his legs were not broken and his side was pierced (19:31-37). If John's quotations of Scripture are numerous only in the Passion story, it is because that part of the career of Jesus was hardest to deify. The Jesus of John needed no divine prediction to support the account of the public ministry, but the crucifixion story could be transformed into the triumph of a god only with the greatest difficulty. To support this transformation the author of the Fourth Gospel turned to the Scriptures.

The creative influence of the Scriptures upon the details of the Passion narrative is well known from the account of

[68] In John 1:45; 2:17; 5:39-40, 46; 6:45; 7:38, 42.

the triumphal entry in Matthew (21:1-7). Matthew is misled by the parallelism of the Hebrew poetry into supposing that two animals were referred to by the prophet. He therefore seriously states that Jesus ordered two animals to be brought, and that Jesus "seated himself upon them." No artist has felt himself equal to the depiction of such an entry, although the triumphal entry is a common theme in Byzantine art. It is influence of this kind that invented the seamless robe incident at the cross.

In the earlier gospels it is simply stated that the executioners divided Jesus' clothes among them by casting lots.[69] But by the time our Gospel was written, in the 22nd Psalm Christian search of the Scriptures has found the prediction of even this act: "They divided my garments among them, and for my clothing they cast lots."[70] The evangelist's ignorance of the rules of Hebrew poetry made this sound like two distinct acts; his narrative of the fulfillment of the prediction therefore contains two acts—dividing and casting lots. The seamless robe is brought in to explain why two acts were necessary; the executioners were too saving to "divide" the robe. This, says John, was done to fulfill what the Scripture said. Such fulfillment is supplied by Christian defenders of the Passion story, not by Roman soldiers at the cross.[71]

---

[69] Matt. 27:35; Mark 15:24; Luke 23:34.
[70] Ps. 22:18.
[71] Heitmueller, *op. cit.,* p. 849 (or 3rd ed., IV, 173).

There are many distinctive details of the Passion story in John that combine to make the story of the death of Jesus more dignified, more fitting for a god, more triumphant. The taunting and jeering at the crucified find no place in John's account. The theme of the taunts reported by the earlier evangelists was that Jesus claimed to be a Savior of others but could not even save himself. Such a charge presupposes that Jesus did not want to be crucified. John has so clearly shown that Jesus came to earth for the purpose of being crucified that he is consistent when he omits this charge from the story of the death.

The omission of the taunt scene was easy for him also in that it made the death scene more dignified. That John was interested in increasing the dignity of Jesus' departure is shown by his failure to label the two who were crucified with Jesus as "criminals" or "robbers."

The superscription in three languages was undoubtedly intended to suggest the function of Jesus as a world Savior. The protest of the Jews against the content of the superscription reminds the reader once more that it was the Jews, *not* the Romans, who were Jesus' enemies.

There are a number of details in the Johannine Passion that remove the story altogether from the category of tragedy. As John interprets the death of Jesus, it was triumph and exaltation for Jesus. The concomitants of misery and tragedy are, therefore, absent from his narrative. He shows us a Jesus who, having already conquered the cosmos,[72] now completes his mission and begins his exaltation by being crucified. He has no despairing cry from the forsaken Jesus, reproaching the Father for abandoning him. In the earlier accounts, the result of this cry was that a bystander ran to get Jesus a drink.[73] John knows that Jesus was not forsaken and that he could not have cried, "My God, my God, why have you forsaken me?" Why, then, did the bystander offer Jesus a drink? Because Jesus had called out, "I am thirsty."[74] Not that he just happened to be thirsty—but rather because Jesus, aware that the last detail of the plan was finished, said this that the Scripture might be fulfilled.[75] Nor was there any loud cry from Jesus at the moment of his death, as Matthew and Mark report. On the contrary, Jesus in the leading role in the drama of redemption closes the scene with the pronouncement, "It is finished."[76]

The interpretation of the crucifixion as triumph rather than tragedy leads John to omit such miracles as the Synoptics report to have accompanied the death of Jesus. There is in John's story no eclipse, no supernatural tearing of the temple veil, no earthquake or resurrection of the dead when

[72] John 16:33.
[73] Mark 15:34-36; Matt. 27:46-49.
[74] John 19:26.
[75] Ps. 69:21 f.
[76] John 19:30.

Jesus dies.[77] Such portents are signs of gloom and dread disaster; nature mourns in sympathy with the suffering and death of Jesus.[78] In the Fourth Gospel there is no excuse for mourning; Jesus experiences crucifixion as a triumph.

Entirely consistent with this is the story of Jesus' assigning his mother to the care of the beloved disciple. Whatever may be intended as the symbolic message of the incident, it definitely suggests that the crucified Jesus was still the Leader and Director. He calmly gives directions for the future care of his mother within a few moments of his own death. The placidity of the incident helps to establish the dominant tone of the Johannine Passion as one of dignity. That Jesus was the most important person of the three executed that day had been suggested by earlier accounts which located his cross in the middle. John retains this tradition; and, in the account of the breaking of the legs, he reports that the soldiers broke the legs of the first man, that they then walked past Jesus to the other, and finally came to Jesus. This reservation of Jesus to the last is one more minor detail to suggest the importance of Jesus in the story.

The same suggestion of importance is given in the burial story. There is in John no suggestion of hurried, incomplete and temporary burial. In John the myrrh-bearing women

[77] Mark 15:33, 38; Matt. 27:51-53.

[78] S. J. Case, *Experience with the Supernatural in Early Christian Times* (New York, 1929), pp. 71-76.

are anticipated. Two of the leading men of the Jewish nation bury Jesus in royal, or perhaps divine, fashion. Nicodemus supplies a hundred pounds of myrrh and aloes for the burial, a munificent contribution. It must be remembered that Christian accounts of the burial of Jesus would be measured by the pagan populace against the presentation of the burial of various deities in mystery cult practice. That such presentations were magnificent spectacles is suggested by the promise made to a follower of magic that his body would be buried in a manner "fitting for a god."[79]

It may be pointed out that the resurrection appearances in John meet with much less incredulity from the disciples than in the earlier gospels. The beloved disciple believes; Mary's message is not disbelieved; the ten believe gladly, and the doubts of Thomas supply the opportunity for a strong encomium of those who believe without seeing. In the Fourth Gospel, Jesus dies like a god, is buried like a god and returns in glory to God his Father.

[79] K. Preisendanz, *P. Gr. Mag. I,* lines 177-79 (Leipzig and Berlin, 1928), p. 10; Goodspeed and Colwell, *op. cit.,* p. 79.

V

The Descent of the Spirit

THE preceding chapter has shown that the Fourth Gospel writer presents Jesus throughout as a divine being. This fact raises important questions as to the Gospel writer's viewpoint on the method of transition from the pre-existent status with the Father to that of the earthly situation; also whether or not Jesus' divine nature is conceived in more specifically Christian terms than the phrase "divine being" would suggest. The answers to these questions, we are convinced, are to be found in the concept of the Spirit's descent upon Jesus at the baptism.

The consensus of scholarly opinion is that the descent of the Spirit in the Fourth Gospel account is a sign to John the Baptist of the Messiahship of Jesus; this is its exclusive function. The writer of the Gospel, it is affirmed, did not intend to suggest that anything happened to Jesus. A statement by a noted author will illustrate this position:

For the author of John, Jesus is not the adopted Son of Ps. 2:7, but the "only Son who is in the bosom of the Father," the pre-existent, eternal Logos. Hence, the descent of the Spirit at his baptism cannot signify that Jesus was now first "anointed with power." It can only be the sign given for the special benefit of the Baptist.[1]

This assumption needs examination. The problem is whether the evangelist intended to suggest that with the Spirit's descent *something happened to Jesus.*

The crucial passage is 1:29-34.

The next day he saw Jesus coming toward him, and said, "Behold, the Lamb of God, who takes away the sin of the world! This is he of whom I said, 'After me comes a man who ranks before me, for he was before me.' I myself did not know him; but for this I came baptizing with water, that he might be revealed to Israel." And John bore witness, "I saw the Spirit descend as a dove from heaven, and it remained on him. I myself did not know him; but he who sent me to baptize with water said to me, 'He on whom you see the Spirit descend and remain, this is he who baptizes with the Holy Spirit.' And I have seen and have borne witness that this is the Son of God."[2]

That the descent of the Spirit contributed something to Jesus is strongly suggested by the declaration of John: "I saw the Spirit descend as a dove from heaven, and it *remained* on him."[3] It is important to note that the Spirit not only

[1] B. W. Bacon, *The Gospel of the Hellenists* (New York: Henry Holt and Company, 1933), p. 157. This is essentially the position of Bultmann who sees the baptism solely as recognition by John, and attributes the contrast between baptizing *in water* (1:26, 31, 33) and "the One who baptizes in the Holy Spirit" (1:34) to the work of the Editor.—*Das Evangelium des Johannes,* p. 63, n. 6.
[2] New Testament quotations in this chapter, unless otherwise indicated, are from the Revised Standard Version.
[3] John 1:32.

identified the Son of God by its descent but also remained on Jesus, a feature of the account which is irrelevant to the function of identification. It seems probable that the writer is combining in the narrative two ideas: first, that at the baptism Jesus became Son of God through the descent of the Spirit; second, that John the Baptist was witness to the event.

In the Gospel according to the Hebrews there appears an interesting account of the descent of the Spirit which may throw light on the Johannine passage.[4] It is reported by Jerome as follows:

[The Spirit of the Lord shall rest upon him] not partially as in the case of other holy men: but, according to the Gospel written in the Hebrew speech, which the Nazarenes read, "There shall descend upon him the whole fount of the Holy Spirit". . . . In the Gospel I mentioned above, I find this written: And it came to pass when the Lord was come up out of the water, the whole fount of the Holy Spirit descended and rested upon him, and said unto him: My son, in all the prophets was I waiting for thee that thou shouldst come, and I might rest in thee. For thou art my rest, thou art my first begotten son, that reignest for ever.[5]

There are obvious similarities between this and the Johannine account. In the former, there descends upon Jesus the "whole fount of the Holy Spirit," while in the latter the

[4] This is not to imply a direct relationship between the two passages but rather to suggest ideas of the Spirit and its relationship to Jesus current in the general period of our gospel.

[5] M. R. James, *The Apocryphal New Testament*, p. 5.

Spirit is not given "by measure."[6] In the apocryphal account there is reference to Jesus as the "first begotten," while in the New Testament gospel Jesus is known as the "only begotten." The "remaining" of the Spirit on Jesus is a feature common to both.

There is no account of the baptism of Jesus, as such, in the Fourth Gospel. For the evangelist the baptism has taken place before its final mention in 1:20. The Baptist is looking into the past at the identification scene; he views the baptism in retrospect. He did not know that Jesus was the Lamb of God *until* he saw the Spirit descend and remain upon him. But he knew this in 1:29. Therefore, the Spirit had already descended upon Jesus in some earlier incident unrecorded in John.

The Gospel writer felt it necessary to explain certain aspects of the tradition about Jesus' baptism: (1) It had been at the hands of John. This embarrassing fact is dealt with by the "witness" device. (2) In the Synoptic accounts, Jesus had been called "Son of God" by the voice from heaven.[7] This he interprets to mean that Jesus at that time was born from above or born of the Spirit. This emphasis is close to that of Mark. But while for Mark it is adoptionism, for the Fourth

[6] The statement that the Spirit was not given to Jesus "by measure" does not appear, it is true, in the statement by the Baptist quoted above. It appears in the third chapter and is also the "witness" of John.

[7] Mark 1:11; Matt. 3:17; Luke 3:22.

Gospel writer it is incarnationism. It appears that in common with Mark, he had no theory of a supernatural birth. He is, therefore, driven to account for the divine nature of Jesus in another manner; the descent of the Spirit at the baptism is his answer.

If what has been said is true, then the descent of the Spirit is of crucial importance in the thought of the Fourth Gospel. It means that in this event lies the real beginning of the Johannine story of Jesus the Son of God; that prior to this, Jesus was the man from Nazareth and nothing more; that the ministry of the Son of God can only begin subsequent to the Spirit's descent when this man from Nazareth has been infused with and transformed by the Holy Spirit in such a way that he has become a divine being. The name "Jesus" is still used but the human characteristics of the *man* Jesus no longer remain except in external appearance. What is essential is the Spirit. Wherever the name "Jesus" is used in the Gospel, the term "Spirit" could be substituted with no real loss in thought. The term "Jesus" does serve to make this divine essence more concretely historical; it is there in visible human form. But the Spirit is the dominant concern.

Is there any evidence that with the baptism this change had taken place? In 1:31, John the Baptist declares that he did not know Jesus prior to the descent of the Spirit. In what sense did he not know him? Did he not know him at all?

Or is the meaning that he did not know him as Messiah? Probably the latter.[8] But was this failure to recognize Jesus as Messiah due to John's incapacity to appreciate what was already there or was it because Jesus' Messianic character had not yet become an accomplished fact? The latter possibility is rarely discussed. The failure to discuss it may be attributed to undue attention to the prologue with its doctrine of the Logos or to the assumption that the writer accepted the birth stories of Matthew and Luke. But a moment's consideration will suffice to show that the prologue does not offer a suggestion as to how the transition of the Logos from the eternal realm to the temporal is effected. And, as will be shown below, the evidence for attributing to the writer the idea of a supernatural birth is completely negative.[9]

There is a passage, the significance of which is obscured by its close association with the first miracle at Cana of Galilee. It is found in 2:1-4. This comes at the very beginning of the public ministry of Jesus. This little section not only serves to introduce the first of the signs but also has significance in its own right. The point of these verses is the repudiation of a filial relationship. τί ἐμοὶ καὶ σοί (literally,

[8] Macgregor thinks the meaning is that John did not recognize Jesus as Messiah, "though probably the two were acquainted as friends." He assumes that Jesus was already Messiah prior to the baptism; that the baptism provides John with evidence of the fact. The attempt to read history into the passage is open to question. See Macgregor, *op. cit.*, p. 30.

[9] See pp. 116-18.

"What to me and to you"), may well be translated, "What do we have in common?" It indicates a change in relationship between Jesus and his mother at the very beginning of his ministry. But why would this be so unless, in the thought of the writer, something had happened at that time to provide a basis for the repudiation?

In this case, as elsewhere, the writer is interpreting history. The historical base here is the fact of estrangement between Jesus and his family during his public career, an unmistakable aspect of the Synoptic tradition. Yet it is equally clear that after the death of Jesus the family became prominent in the Christian church. The Fourth Gospel writer is extremely creative in his interpretation of these facts: When Jesus entered upon his ministry as divine Son of God he ceased to be subject to his mother. He was no longer son of a mortal woman but divine Son of God. Former relationships no longer held true.

This explains the writer's use of the word γύναι (woman). Attempts have been made to soften the word. These attempts have led to various translations, such as "mother" and "lady" —surely ill-advised—while other translators have omitted the English equivalent altogether. It may be admitted that the Greek γύναι is not as harsh as the English "woman," but it is none the less a formal designation. The fact is that even the Jesus of the Synoptics does not go out of his way to speak tenderly of his mother. The situation is quite the contrary as the following passages indicate:

And his mother and his brothers came; and standing outside they sent to him and called him. And a crowd was sitting about him; and they said to him, "Your mother and your brothers are outside, asking for you." And he answered, "Who are my mother and my brothers? . . . Whoever does the will of God is my brother, and sister, and mother."[10]

"If any one comes to me and does not hate his own father and mother and wife and children and brothers and sisters, yes, and even his own life, he cannot be my disciple."[11]

Now the Johannine Jesus would be far less likely to use words of family endearment than the Synoptic Jesus, for in the Fourth Gospel Jesus is the majestic Son of God, who, while he is in the world, is in no sense a part of it. His sayings are not on the level of ordinary human discourse, but are pronouncements of a divine being.[12] At the outset, therefore, Jesus serves notice that he is different from the ordinary run of mankind. Relationships which apply to them do not apply to him. This holds true for his entire ministry.

The words "My hour has not yet come" are important in this connection. The "hour" of the Fourth Gospel is the hour of Jesus' death. Is it a mere coincidence that not until

[10] Mark 3:31-35.

[11] Luke 14:26-27.

[12] The word γύναι was used in an additional sense to indicate a mortal woman as opposed to a divine goddess. This may well be the meaning in the Johannine passage. 2:4a would then read: "Mortal woman, what have we in common?"

the "hour" has come do we again find him in conversation with his mother and in this second conversation *establishing* a filial relationship?[13] To be sure, it is with the disciple whom Jesus loved, but that disciple is as near to Jesus as anyone can be and yet maintain a separate existence. When this act is completed, Jesus recognizes that all is finished and yields up his spirit. Thus the two events span the ministry, and at the end the mother of Jesus is safely within the fold of the Christian fellowship.

This interpretation of the historical estrangement between Jesus and his family is not far wide of the mark. Historically, his own family could not appreciate who he was or what he was doing. Actually, he lived in a world remote from theirs. It was this that caused the estrangement to take place; a not uncommon cause of tragic alienation in human relationships. But subsequent developments apparently enabled them to understand, at least to some degree, the meaning of his strange commitment, and they became his followers. Human history testifies to the fact that only slowly do the masses of men come to understand the strange compulsions of those individuals who are sensitive to a higher world of meaning. But the point to note is that the writer recognizes a change in Jesus' relationship with those who are "of this

[13] John 19:26-27.

world," which argues for a corresponding difference in Jesus himself..

The problem of Jesus' nature prior to the descent of the Spirit may be investigated in relation to the problem of his origin. There are two recurrent themes in the Gospel of John: (1) "Where did he come from?" (2) "Where is he going?" These raise the problem of his origin and destiny. Involved in the question of his origin is the matter of his true identity. The Gospel maintains that his true nature is contingent on his true origin; if his true origin can be shown his true nature will be revealed. The Jews think they know his origin (they know his family); hence, they cannot understand how he can rightfully claim to be more than a son of Joseph. How could he legitimately say, "I am the Son of God," or "I have come down from heaven"?

It is, therefore, a striking fact that the writer nowhere argues for the Messiahship of Jesus either on the basis of Davidic descent or of a supernatural birth. In this gospel, Jesus is a Galilean, and Joseph is his father.[14] The passages containing these ideas are, it may be objected, the statements of Jesus' enemies and so cannot be taken seriously. There is a threefold answer to this. In the first place, Philip and Nathanael, who are involved in the earliest passage, can scarcely be called enemies of Jesus. In the second place, the

[14] John 1:45; 6:41-42; 7:40-42.

nature of the Fourth Gospel as thoroughgoing composition makes it possible for the writer to refute any notion with which he does not agree. He nowhere refutes these ideas. Finally, and most significantly, on the level of these ideas of place of physical birth and mode of physical birth the Jews of the Fourth Gospel must be granted accuracy. It is on this level that they are at home. It is sometimes said that the Jews are always wrong in the Gospel of John. The fact is that the Jews are usually right *but on an entirely physical level of understanding.* Nicodemus is right regarding the impossibility of physical rebirth. The Jews are right when they ridicule the idea that one not yet fifty years of age could have seen Abraham; they are right when they suggest that it is impossible for Jesus to give them his flesh to eat; they are right when they say that they know where he comes from; they are right when they say they know his father and mother.

The strength of the Johannine argument is due in large part to the accuracy of these observations and others like them. They are all true enough but are observations on the physical level. What the Jews cannot understand are the spiritual counterparts of these obvious "facts": the birth from above, the eternal nature of the Son of God, the spiritual meaning of Jesus as Bread of Life, the heavenly origin of Jesus, and his true parentage in God. These are the important truths for the writer. It follows, then, that he can have Jesus born a Galilean, as the son of Joseph, for this is of minor consequence in comparison with the fact that he has come down from heaven, and that through the descent of the Spirit, he has been born from above. His divine nature is due, not to Davidic descent nor to the paternity of Joseph, but to the Spirit of God which came upon him at the baptism. The statement, "That which is born of the flesh is flesh, and that which is born of the Spirit is spirit," is just as true for Jesus as for those who by virtue of the Spirit's bestowal at a later time were to be born from above.

Jesus has, in John, a dual origin: Nazareth and heaven. This dual origin provides the explanation of the problematical passage, John 4:43-45:

> After the two days he [Jesus] departed to Galilee. For Jesus himself testified that a prophet has no honor in his own country. So when he came to Galilee, the Galileans welcomed him, having seen all that he had done in Jerusalem at the feast, for they too had gone to the feast.

The problem grows out of the fact that the passage implies that Judea and not Galilee is Jesus' "own country." But in the Synoptics, Galilee (specifically Nazareth) is so designated. And there can be little doubt that the evangelist is using the Synoptic passage as a source.

From the strictly human point of view Jesus' own country

is Nazareth and Galilee. Passages which support this assertion are the following:

Philip found Nathanael, and said to him, "We have found him
of whom Moses in the law and also the prophets wrote, Jesus of
Nazareth, the son of Joseph." Nathanael said to him, "Can
anything good come out of Nazareth?" Philip said to him,
"Come and see." [1:45-46]

The Jews then murmured at him, because he said, "I am the
bread which came down from heaven." They said, "Is not this
Jesus, the son of Joseph, whose father and mother we know?
How does he now say, 'I have come down from heaven?'" [6:41-
42]

It should be noted that the locale of this incident is Galilee:
Galilean Jews know Jesus' parents.

When they heard these words, some of the people said, "This
is really the prophet." Others said, "This is the Christ." But some
said, "Is the Christ to come from Galilee? Has not the scripture
said that the Christ is descended from David, and comes from
Bethlehem, the village where David was?" So there was a
division among the people over him. [7:40-43]

The implication of this passage is that the Jews knew Jesus
to be from Galilee.

Nicodemus . . . said to them, "Does our law judge a man
without first giving him a hearing and learning what he does?"
They replied, "Are you from Galilee too? Search and you will
see that no prophet is to rise from Galilee." [7:50-52]

A few additional passages contain the stereotyped "Jesus of Nazareth." These are 18:5, 7; 19:19.

These references indicate clearly that John held to a Galilean origin of Jesus. The point is that Jesus *as a human being* came from Nazareth. Philip, already a disciple of Jesus, makes the assertion. And the testimony of the Jews to physical matters is accurate; they know him only as Jesus of Galilee.

But in a deeper sense Jesus' own country is not Galilee but heaven. The assertion that he has come down from heaven is made repeatedly. The following are representative examples: "For I have come down from heaven, not to do my own will, but the will of him who sent me" (6:38). "Jesus said to them, 'If God were your Father, you would love me, for I proceeded and came forth from God'" (8:42). "I came from the Father and have come into the world" (16:28). This is also the meaning of the numerous passages which refer to Jesus as the "one sent" from God.[15] This heavenly origin of Jesus must be understood in terms of the descent of the Spirit at the baptism. When this heavenly Jesus speaks it is never of his human parentage or geographical origin, but of his pre-existence with his Father in heaven. The Jesus who came from heaven is Jesus as the Spirit.

[15] 3:17, 34; 5:23, 30; 6:29, 38, 44, 57; 7:16, 18, 28, 33; 8:18, 26, 29, 42; 12:44, 45, 49; 13:20, etc.

THE DESCENT OF THE SPIRIT

Now it is Jesus as the Spirit which makes possible the designation of Judea and Jerusalem as Jesus' own country. For one thing, Jesus as the Spirit is Jesus as the Christ conceived, of course, in uniquely Johannine terms.[16] His association with Jerusalem therefore becomes a necessity for that is where the Messiah ought to appear. This alone is sufficient to account for the fact that the writer has shifted Jesus' main center of activity from Galilee to Jerusalem. It reveals the fallacy of the attempt to find historical support in John for a three-year ministry. The interest of the fourth evangelist is dogmatic not historical. In his role as the Christ, Jesus properly belongs to Jerusalem; it is his own country.

The Gospel writer's view of the cross provides a second reason why he relates Jesus to Jerusalem. Jesus belongs to Jerusalem because that is where he is to be crucified. All that is involved in the seven signs and in the discourses comes to a sharp focus in the cross; by it Jesus is glorified; it is the judgment seat; it is the agent in the universalizing of the Spirit. For our author, as well as for Luke, it cannot

[16] The concept of Jesus as the Spirit, in fact, accounts for the many titles for Jesus which the fourth evangelist employs. "Jesus," of course, is the basic historical name which all early Christian writers use in some form (e.g., "Jesus," "Jesus Christ," "Christ Jesus," "Jesus Christ our Lord," "The Lord Jesus Christ"). Strangely enough this most "historical" name becomes in a sense the least fitting in our Gospel, for the historical person is virtually eclipsed by a super-earthly being. The name "Jesus" is carried along by the sheer force of the historical fact. However, behind all other terms applied to Jesus in this Gospel lies the Spirit concept. It accounts for Jesus as Christ, Son of God, Son of Man, Lord, Savior, and God.

be that a prophet perish away from Jerusalem. It is where Jesus belongs; it is his own country. Jesus as a man is from Nazareth, Jesus as the Spirit-filled Christ belongs to Jerusalem. And it is the latter emphasis which is the almost complete concern of the Gospel writer.

This emphasis on Jesus as the Spirit is apparent throughout the Gospel. The word δόξα (glory) indicates that his nature is identical with that of the Father: "We have seen his glory, glory as of the only-begotten Son from the Father" (1:14). The first miracle at Cana (2:1-11) illustrates his spiritual nature. The raising of Lazarus is a manifestation of God's glory in terms of the Resurrection and the Life (11:41). But this also indicates the true nature of Jesus (11:24); God's nature and Jesus' nature are identical. The passage, " 'Father, glorify thy name.' Then a voice came from heaven, 'I have glorified it, and I will glorify it again' " (12:28), speaks of two glorifications, one as past and one as future. The former is possibly an allusion to the manifestation in the seven signs, but more probably is a reference to the descent of the Spirit at the baptism, when Jesus became filled with the Spirit. The signs are evidences of his glory, the descent of the Spirit makes these possible, (17:22), so is itself a glorification. The glorification yet to come is clearly an allusion to the crucifixion (17:1), and its attendant circumstance of exaltation (17:5), and the gift of the Spirit to the disciples (17:22; 20:22-23).[17]

The seven signs of the first eleven chapters are attempts on the part of the Spirit-filled Jesus to manifest his true identity to the unbelieving Jews. The Cana of Galilee incident of the changing of water into wine illustrates this. The incident is reminiscent of the Pentecost story of Acts. In the Acts account the Spirit-filled disciples are accused of being "filled with new wine" (2:13). But Peter assures the crowd that this is not the case; instead they are filled with the Spirit as Joel has predicted: "And in the last days it shall be, God says, that I will pour out my Spirit on all flesh" (2:16-17). In the same manner Jesus gives the Spirit in the Cana story to replace the inferior religion of the Jews. In the Acts account the Spirit comes unto them "like the rush of a mighty wind, and it filled all the house where they were sitting" (2:2). Similarly, in the Johannine story Jesus gives the wine in lavish quantities. He does this to manifest his glory, i.e., his true nature. Thus in the very first incident the evangelist makes it clear that Jesus is essentially different. In Mark, Jesus is under control of the Spirit (it throws him out into the desert) at the outset of

[17] Bultmann in commenting on 20:19-23 (though he is preoccupied with his hypothetical source and what the evangelist has done with it) still at last recognizes the importance of the gift of the Spirit as intended to fulfill the promises of the Farewell Discourses.

his ministry (1:12). In John, this is never so. Jesus is spirit so that all he has to do is to reveal the fact.

A second illustration of Jesus as the Spirit is the Nicodemus story (3:1-21). The story begins with Nicodemus' statement to Jesus: "Rabbi, we know that you are a teacher come from God; for no one can do these signs that you do, unless God is with him." Then in typically Johannine fashion Jesus replies with a cryptic remark: "Amen, amen I say to you, unless one is born *anōthen* [from above], he cannot see the Kingdom of God."[18] Notice that Nicodemus' statement raises the question of Jesus' origin. He is a teacher who has come from God: this is the source of his ability to perform signs. At first glance it would appear that Jesus has shifted the basis of argument with his reply about being born *anōthen*. This, however, is not so. Jesus' reference to the necessity of birth from above applies to him as well as to Nicodemus. Indeed, apart from Jesus' own birth from above there could be no such experience for Nicodemus, or for others: "That which is born of the flesh is flesh, and that which is born of the Spirit is spirit." This is the same emphasis as that of the discourse on the bread of life: "the flesh profits nothing" (6:63). In the latter case, the reference is to eating Jesus' flesh. For the evangelist physical birth is of minor import. As the Spirit-filled Son of God, Jesus speaks

---

[18] Translation ours.

of heavenly things which are beyond the Jews: "He who is of the earth belongs to the earth and of the earth he speaks; he who comes from heaven is above all" (3:31).

The great difference between Jesus and other men is that Jesus is first in the succession; as such he is the mediator of the Spirit. Apart from him the experience of the Church could not have been possible. It is instructive to note the similarity between this concept and that of Paul in 1 Corinthians, chapter fifteen:

What is sown is perishable, what is raised is imperishable. . . . It is sown a physical body, it is raised a spiritual body. Thus it is written, "The first man Adam became a living being"; the last Adam became a life-giving Spirit. But it is not the spiritual which is first but the physical, and then the spiritual. The first man was from the earth, a man of dust; the second man is from heaven. As was the man of dust, so are those who are of the dust; and as is the man of heaven, so are those who are of heaven. Just as we have borne the image of the man of dust, we shall also bear the image of the man of heaven. I tell you this, brethren: flesh and blood cannot inherit the kingdom of God, nor does the perishable inherit the imperishable.

Of course Paul entertained an eschatological point of view which makes for superficial differences. But the Fourth Gospel writer reads the same essential affirmation back into the lifetime of Jesus. As Dr. E. J. Goodspeed had said, "The Gospel of John begins where Paul left off."[19]

[19] E. J. Goodspeed, *A Life of Jesus* (New York: Harper & Brothers, 1950), p. 227.

An important section for consideration is 3:31-36.

He who comes from above is above all; he who is of the earth belongs to the earth, and of the earth he speaks; he who comes from heaven is above all. He bears witness to what he has seen and heard, yet no one receives his testimony; he who receives his testimony sets his seal to this, that God is true. For he whom God has sent utters the words of God, for it is not by measure that he gives the Spirit; the Father loves the Son, and has given all things into his hand. He who believes in the Son has eternal life; he who does not obey the Son shall not see life, but the wrath of God rests upon him.

It is a statement by John the Baptist, but there is no doubt that it is about Jesus. Note the use of *anōthen* in this connection: "He who comes *anōthen* is above all." It is the same word used by Jesus in his conversation with Nicodemus. Furthermore, Jesus has received the Spirit without measure: "For he whom God has sent utters the words of God, for it is not by measure that he gives the Spirit." The meaning is not that God gives the Spirit without measure to anyone, but that he so gives it to Jesus: "The Father loves the Son and has given all things into his hand."

The allusion to the "seal" in this passage may have some relation to the bestowal of the Spirit. There is little doubt that this is the intention of the use of the word in 6:27, "Do not labor for the food which perishes, but for the food which endures to eternal life, which the Son of man will

give to you; for on him has God the Father *set his seal*."[20]
What is this "seal" which God has placed upon Jesus? The
answer is found in the Christian concept of the Holy Spirit:
"But it is God who establishes us with you in Christ, and
has commissioned us; he has put his seal upon us and given
us his Spirit in our hearts as a guarantee" (2 Cor. 1:21-22).
Ephesians has two similar references: "In him you also, who
have heard the word of truth, the gospel of your salvation,
and have believed in him, were sealed with the promised
Holy Spirit, which is the guarantee of our inheritance until
we acquire possession of it, to the praise of his glory" (1:13-
14). "And do not grieve the Holy Spirit of God, in whom
you were sealed for the day of redemption" (4:30). Likewise, in the Fourth Gospel the coming of the Spirit upon
Jesus is God's seal upon him. Again, Jesus is the first in the
series of those upon whom the Spirit came, making the experience of the church possible.

The Samaritan woman story (4:1-26) speaks of the true
nature of Jesus under the figure of "living water." That this
figure means that Jesus is Spirit is shown by the reference
in 7:37-39:

On the last day of the feast, the great day, Jesus stood up and
proclaimed, "If any one thirst, let him come to me and drink.
He who believes in me, as the scripture has said, 'Out of his

[20] Italics ours.

heart shall flow rivers of living water.'" Now this he said about the Spirit, which those who believed in him were to receive; for as yet the Spirit had not been given, because Jesus was not yet glorified.

The term "living water" is equivalent to life-giving Spirit (cf. 5:21; 5:25; 6:63; 1 Cor. 15:45).

In the story, Jesus leads the woman from one level of meaning to another. He asks for a drink. This initiates the action of the story. The woman is puzzled by Jesus' request in view of the historic feud between Samaritans and Jews. This gives Jesus opportunity to pronounce on his own nature: "If you knew the gift of God and who it is that is saying to you, 'Give me a drink,' you would have asked him, and he would have given you living water." The woman is still ignorant of Jesus' meaning. She thinks he is speaking of spring water as opposed to cistern water. Does he have access to water superior to that of which Jacob and his household drank? This again enables Jesus to speak of his own nature: "Every one who drinks of this water will thirst again, but whoever drinks of the water that I shall give him will never thirst; the water that I shall give him will become in him a spring of water welling up to eternal life."[21]

[21] It is interesting to observe that while in the introductory part of the story (4:4-6) Jacob's well is called a πηγή (spring), in the narrative the woman refers to it as a ὕδωρ (cistern). Here is another Johannine play on words for when Jesus contrasts the well water with the living water which he bestows he uses the term meaning "spring." It is the contrast between stagnant water and fresh, running water. The latter suggests his true nature.

A transition takes place in this part of the account. Jesus tells the Samaritan woman to call her husband. She replies that she has no husband. This leads to Jesus' statement that she has had five husbands, and that the one she now has is not her huband. There may be symbolism here,[22] but in the structure of the account it makes possible the climax of the story which is Jesus' pronouncement on the nature of God and of true worship. The nature of God is spirit (4:24). This simple statement has been underemphasized in studies of the Fourth Gospel. It ought to be taken seriously. Since spirit is God's nature, worship of God is not dependent on place, whether Jerusalem or Mount Gerizim. The evangelist here, as always, is speaking to his contemporaries. This statement and a later one belong together: "Have you believed because you have seen me? Blessed are those who have not seen and yet believe" (20:29). The climactic statement of the story comes in 4:25-26, after the reference to God as Spirit:

The woman said to him, "I know that Messiah is coming (he who is called Christ); when he comes, he will show us all things." Jesus said to her, "I who speak to you am he."

The entire story is a witness to the nature of Jesus as the Spirit. God is spirit and Jesus as one sent from God is the Spirit. What was suggested by the phrase "living water" is

[22] See pp. 60-64.

merely made explicit by the definition of God as spirit. Jesus and the Father are of one nature.

The role of John the Baptist as inferior underscores the emphasis on Jesus as the Spirit also; it sets Jesus apart in a higher category. The writer begins with a ruthlessly negative definition of the Baptist himself. The prologue of the Gospel is interrupted by the assurance that John was not the Light, but only one of his witnesses, sent to the world to announce the greater one (1:6, 15). When an official embassy from Jerusalem asks John what he is, he replies that he is nothing but a herald, a broadcaster of the arrival of the Messiah (1:19-23). The outstanding feature of John's reply is its negative nature as regards John himself. "He confessed and did not deny; and he confessed" is the language of the Christian apologist, not of the rugged prophet of the desert whose explanation of himself would have rung with robust pride in his mission. Negatives dominate the whole conversation. "I am *not* the Messiah." Are you Elijah? "I am *not!*" Are you the prophet? "*No!*" By this series of denials the sensational herald of the Kingdom, the popular preacher of penitence, the founder of a cult and ritual, becomes nothing but a voice. The gap between Jesus and John is wide and deep.

This voice, in the Fourth Gospel, has but one mission— to identify Jesus publicly as the Savior of the world—the one on whom the Spirit came. When John has done this he has fulfilled his task in the divine scheme of things (1:24-34). Therefore, there is here no mention of the exhortation to repentance, no mention of sins, no mention of the actual baptism itself.

As the Baptist explains it, the whole situation has the unreality of the stage. John had been sent into the world so that he might point out the Son of God to the world. When John announced the Spirit-filled Jesus his divinely-appointed work was finished. In realization of this, the disciples of John become disciples of Jesus (1:35 f.). The story is so told as to suggest that the Baptist not only acquiesces in this transfer, but even favors it. The force of such a story in controversy between Christians and Baptists cannot be overestimated. In a positive fashion it subordinates John to Jesus; just as the omission of the baptism itself negatively answers the charge that Jesus was subordinate to John.[23] The basis of the subordination is this: Jesus possesses the Spirit, John does not.

As the story is told in this Gospel, Jesus could not be reduced to the role of successor to the Baptist. The sequence of Mark 1:14, "After John was arrested, Jesus went into Galilee," is openly denied in John 3:24, where we are told that Jesus began his ministry before the Baptist was im-

[23] Mark 1:8, and parallels.

prisoned. Since they carried on distinct movements at the same time, Jesus' work could not be regarded as a supplement to John's. This very separateness, however, might have suggested that the Baptist was a dangerous rival of Jesus, if the evangelist had not anticipated such a development and made it impossible. We are told (3:26) that the crowds went to Jesus instead of to John. Jesus was making more disciples than John (4:1). But the fact that Jesus has eclipsed him does not rouse the Baptist to rivalry—not in this story. He accepts what has happened as inevitable for two reasons. First, since he finished his own work with the identification of Jesus, he had expected to become less and less important. Second, he had already identified Jesus in the highest possible categories; therefore, the church (the bride) belonged to Jesus, and he himself could claim significance only inasmuch as he was a friend of Jesus (3:25-30). The whole emphasis is on the superior character of Jesus: Jesus possesses something which makes him greater.

The difference between Jesus and the Baptist is seen also in the inferior quality of the latter's baptism. "I am baptizing only in water," said John (1:26), in a deprecatory answer to the question of why he baptized if he was not a Messianic figure. And the author never lets us forget that John's baptism was "only" water. The question alluded to above was asked "on the farther side of the Jordan, where

John was baptizing" (1:28). It was in order that Jesus might be made known to Israel, says John, "that I have come and baptized people *in water*" (1:31). It is a striking contrast that God who sent John "to baptize *in water*" should make the signal of recognition be the descent of the Spirit on Jesus (1:32-34). John was "baptizing at Aenon, near Salim, for there was plenty of *water* there" (3:23). Jesus on one occasion "went across *the Jordan* again, to the place where John used to baptize at first" (10:40).

Just as this insistence that John's baptism was merely a water baptism indicates the inferior status of the Baptist, so our Gospel's emphasis on the baptism which Jesus gives as being a spiritual baptism indicates Jesus' exalted position. It is true that the antithesis is stated in the earlier gospels.[24] But in John it plays a much more important role.[25] Symbol after symbol is employed by the evangelist to show that Jesus is able to give the Spirit to his followers beyond their heart's desire. Jesus gives the Spirit as he gave the wine in Cana, more richly than a gushing spring. One must be born of water *and the Spirit*. In the conversation with Nicodemus it is the spirit birth that is discussed; the relatively unimportant baptism in water is mentioned and dismissed from the

[24] Mark 1:8, and parallels.
[25] Something approaching the force of the Johannine contrast is found in Acts 18:24-19:7, where the superiority of the Christians to the Baptists lies in their ability to give the Spirit to their converts.

conversation. Jesus himself baptized no one with water (4:1 f.), but he does baptize with the Spirit! For the great climax of the ministry of Jesus in the Fourth Gospel is the scene in which he breathes upon his disciples and says to them, "Receive the Holy Spirit" (20:19-23). In no other gospel does Jesus actually baptize with the Spirit. They all predict that he will, but do not record the fulfillment. The only exception is the story of Pentecost in Acts, where the bestowal of the Spirit is not closely associated with Jesus. In John, that baptism with the Spirit which was Christianity's advantage over the cult of the Baptist is read back into the confines of the Gospel itself. John baptized with water, but Jesus baptized with the Spirit, and only Jesus can do the latter.

The foundation of the evangelist's conviction that Jesus is superior to John is his faith that Jesus is a Spirit-filled being, a god, while John was only a man. But the contrast is openly made in a section whose function is to put Jesus above John (3:22-31). John's recognition of himself as a diminishing power over against the increasing power of Jesus is based on his knowledge that Jesus is divine while he himself is human. "He who comes from above [Jesus] is above all others. A son of earth [John] belongs to earth and speaks of earth. He who comes from heaven is above all others." All Jesus' superiorities to John derive from this one great superiority—a god is superior to a man. And this same passage indicates how Jesus became divine: it was because he had received the Spirit without measure.

A clue to the centrality of the Spirit idea is found in the recurring references to Jesus as *one sent* from God. There are forty-three of these specific references in the Fourth Gospel, and the idea is present in many more passages. This means that Jesus derived his power and knowledge directly from God. This, of course, implies pre-existence. The Spirit comes down and dwells within a man giving an explanation of Jesus in functional terms. The clearest statement of the Fourth Gospel's interpretation of Jesus' pre-existence occurs in 20:21-23:

"As the Father has sent me, even so send I you." And when he had said this, he breathed on them, and said to them, "Receive the Holy Spirit. If you forgive the sins of any, they are forgiven; if you retain the sins of any, they are retained."

Jesus sends them in precisely the same manner in which the Father had sent him. In each case the important thing was the bestowal of the Spirit. Just as the essential thing in him was the Spirit, so now that which is to make the great difference in them will be the possession of the Spirit. The Synoptic question, "Who can forgive sins but God alone?"[26] is answered here. Jesus can forgive sins for he has the Spirit

[26] Mark 2:7; cf. Matt. 2:5; Luke 5:21.

of God and bestows this same power upon the disciples by giving them the Spirit. This is the great climax of the Fourth Gospel. It signifies that for the evangelist the Spirit is the divine pre-existent Jesus and the coming of the Spirit is the coming of Jesus.

The implication of what has been said is that prior to the descent of the Spirit, Jesus of Nazareth was not particularly distinctive. The words of John the Baptist, "I myself did not know him," indicate only that John did not know Jesus as Messiah and Son of God. Prior to this point there was nothing unique about him. The descent of the Spirit made the great change. To be sure, he *appeared* no different after the event: his mother continues to try to exert her authority over him; the Jews think of him as one whose prosaic origin they know. But the fact is that he is essentially different. These two facts, the materialistic aspects of his life and the spiritual event, unknown to the Jews, make for confusion and misunderstanding. The Spirit of God has literally "taken him over," infused his body so that he ceases to be the *man*, Jesus of Nazareth; he is the divine Son of God.

The question now arises as to the significance of all of this for an understanding of the Fourth Gospel.

Any intelligent interpretation of the book must begin, not from the vantagepoint of the lifetime of Jesus but from that of the Gospel writer himself. One must inquire as to his problems and interests. One of his main interests seems to be with the work of the Spirit in the Christian community.

The Acts account is an excellent illustration of this way of viewing Christian history. Christianity's triumphant march from Jerusalem to Rome was contingent on the pouring out of the Spirit at Pentecost (2:1-4). The narrative proceeds on the assumption that this is a divine adventure; human resources and ingenuity fade into the background and disappear. This is the new age foretold by Joel: "And in the last days, God says, I will pour out my Spirit on all flesh." Consequently, speeches in Acts are due to the Holy Spirit (4:8; 4:31; 6:10; 13:9). Christians are the sole possessors of the Spirit (8:18; 19:2-7). It is a great evil to sin against the Holy Spirit (5:1-11). The Holy Spirit directs their activities and makes the victorious westward march of Christianity possible (8:29; 10:19-20; 13:4; 16:6; 20:22; 21:11; 28:25-28).

The evangelist starts with the Spirit's presence as the important item of Christian history. He wants to account for this aspect of Christian experience and its relation to Jesus and to God. He starts with contemporary history and then works back to the period of Jesus. What is his answer?

By virtue of the descent of the Spirit, Jesus is the sole possessor of the Spirit. It is, as it were, compressed and concentrated in him. It is not so much that Jesus *possesses* the Spirit as it is that Jesus *is* the Spirit. He is particularly

(137)

attracted to those passages in Paul which have to do with
an emphasis on spirit. Behind the Nicodemus story seems
to be the great emphasis of 1 Corinthians 15 on Christ as
"life-giving spirit." For this writer, the words of Paul, "The
Lord is the Spirit," are literally true of the Jesus who lived
among men.[27] He is the Son of God because he has been
born from above. His spiritual birth is a special case, the
crucial, all-important link between God and men. "God is
spirit," and as such belongs to an order of reality different
from that of the natural, earthly life. When the Holy Spirit
descends upon Jesus, one step has been taken in bridging the
gap between the world of the spirit and the world of the
flesh. But it is only one step. Jesus is really not of the world
but above it. The Spirit has not yet been mediated to the rest
of men. How can this be accomplished? For this writer, the
death of Jesus is the answer.

Jesus' death releases the Spirit into the world, and becomes
an absolute necessity as the second step in bridging the two
worlds of spirit and flesh. The function of Jesus is that of
mediating the Holy Spirit which properly belongs to the
eternal realm to this temporal realm, which, in a very real
sense, is foreign to its nature. Or perhaps more accurately, it
makes the eternal world available to men now in that it
lifts them above this world of mundane things.

[27] 2 Cor. 3:17.

Contrary to Scott's opinion that the doctrine of the Spirit has no real place in the theology of the gospel as a whole, it is the central and controlling idea.[28] This is seen in connection with the function of the death of Jesus if the return of Christ and the giving of the Spirit are viewed as the same thing. As early as the seventh chapter there is an explicit reference to the function of the Spirit which can be fulfilled only after the death of Jesus:

> On the last day of the feast, the great day, Jesus stood up and proclaimed, "If any one thirst, let him come to me and drink. He who believes in me, as the scripture has said, 'Out of his heart shall flow rivers of living water.'" Now this he said about the Spirit, which those who believed in him were to receive; for as yet the Spirit had not been given, because Jesus was not yet glorified.[29]

The same idea is conveyed by the earlier account of the Samaritan woman, where Jesus says:

> Every one who drinks of this water will thirst again, but whoever drinks of the water that I shall give him will never thirst; the water that I shall give him will become in him a spring of water welling up to eternal life.[30]

This seems to mean that the possession of eternal life is itself contingent on the bestowal of the Spirit and can become a

---

[28] E. F. Scott, *The Fourth Gospel: Its Purpose and Theology*, p. 346.
[29] John 7:37-39.
[30] John 4:13-14.

reality only after Jesus' death. To say, therefore, that eternal
life is a present possession in the Fourth Gospel is correct
only as one takes his position with the writer within the
Christian movement after Jesus' death; not with the contemporary of Jesus who listens to his words. The latter is
limited in what he may expect from Jesus. The great gift of
life is contingent on the cross.

To say this, however, is but to recognize that the real
message of the writer is to his contemporaries. His literary
vehicle being a "gospel," he seems to be dealing with the
situation in Jesus' own time. Since this is so he finds it difficult to be consistent in his account of man's relation to Jesus.
There is both rejection and belief. And even the belief is, for
the most part, not real belief. Those who truly believe are the
disciples and they are a symbol of the church. But it can
scarcely be said that even they find their rightful status apart
from the gift of the Spirit which is future. The disciples
while with Jesus occupy a special place because they have
been chosen out of the world. But when the Spirit of truth
comes he will guide them into all truth.

It may be seen, therefore, that whether one works ahead
from the descent of the Spirit in the first chapter or back
from the bestowal of the Spirit in the last chapter of the
Gospel proper, the result is the same; the emphasis is on

Jesus as possessor of the Spirit. But he receives it only to give it: the great central fact of early Christian experience as reflected in Paul and in the book of Acts. Not only in an allegorical but also in a more literal sense, this is a "spiritual Gospel."

VI

The Revelation of God

"HE who has seen me has seen the Father." This statement is the most explicit mention in the Fourth Gospel of the revelatory function of Jesus. But it merely makes explicit what is everywhere present: Jesus is the revelation of God.

This does not mean, however, that the revelation is conceived in philosophical terms. One group in John's environment which has been given undue attention is the group of Greek philosophers, especially the Stoics. This Gospel has been called "the philosopher's Gospel," and no survey of the Johannine milieu has neglected Stoicism.[1] This over-

[1] This is true from the time of E. F. Scott's work to the present day. Professor C. H. Dodd refers to the Fourth Gospel's "points of contact" with Stoicism, and says, "It is obvious that it [the Gospel] has affinity with Platonic thought." See his stimulating lecture, *The Background of the Fourth Gospel* (reprinted from the "Bulletin of the John Rylands Library," Vol. 19, No. 2, July, 1935 [Manchester, 1935]), pp. 10 f. But John is not using "real bread," "real vine," and "real light," in a Platonic sense—however remote. The contrast is not one between "phenomenal" and "ideal," but between Christian and non-Christian. Jesus—not the Baptist—was the real light; Jesus—not the manna, or Judaism— was the real bread from heaven; Jesus—not Dionysus, or Manda d'Haije, or any other Hellenistic savior—was the real vine. The context makes this inescapably plain in the first two cases. Walter Bauer tentatively suggests that John's use of "real" (i.e., "true") is colored in part by the influence of the noun "truth" upon him.—*Das Johannesevangelium* (3rd ed., Tuebingen, 1933), on 1:9.

emphasis springs from the use of a technical Stoic term—the Logos, or Reason—in the prologue of the Gospel. The important use of this term by the apologists and creedmakers has so colored the thinking of the Christian reader that he sees the whole Gospel in the light of this one word in the first line. This is the most common and far-reaching perversion of the Gospel in present-day study.

The relative unimportance of the term "Logos" for the fourth evangelist can be seen in the fact that his use of it is due to a literary heritage. The prologue existed in a briefer, non-Christian form before the evangelist took it up and re-shaped it to serve as an introduction to his Gospel. That the presence of John the Baptist in verses 6-8 and 15 is due to editorial work, revising a hymn to Light, Life, Truth and Grace, is obvious. That the hand that supplied these verses is the hand of the evangelist is equally plain. The natural conclusion is that the original prologue is not from the hand of the evangelist.[2] The specifically Christian content of the prologue (aside from the anti-Baptist verses) occurs in part of verse 14 and in verses 17-18. The rest of the material most probably comes from a hymn to some Revealer of the Truth which was composed in a Gnostic cult that had nothing to

---

[2] Unless we accept the ingenious suggestion of Grant that the author of the gospel is rewriting his own youthful hymn to the Logos—*The Growth of the Gospels* (New York, 1931). But this hypothesis hardly does justice to the prominence of Life-Light-Truth-Grace in the prologue.

do with Christianity and very little with Stoicism.[3] From Stoicism it had taken the term "Logos" as its link with antiquity and divinity, both in creation and revelation. But the important words in the original prologue were "Life," "Light," "Truth," "Fullness" and "Grace," not "Reason."

The reappearance of most of these important words in the Gospel itself is explained by the supposition that John took this prologue material from the religious group which so strongly influenced his entire conception of religion as Revelation, Life, Light and Truth. The alien origin of the prologue can still be recognized through its use of the non-Johannine words "Logos," "Fullness" and "Grace." None of these words occurs in the Gospel in the sense in which they are used here; "logos" is used—but not of a divine being or power. The word "grace," which formed the climax of the original prologue, is never used in the Gospel, nor is the idea expressed in other words. The "fullness" is likewise non-Johannine. In these three words the prologue is much closer to Paul than to John, and it would be rash to assume that any one of these words led John to the use of this prologue. It was the presence of the Light-Life-Truth concepts that attracted John to this document, which he rewrote into closer conformity with his purposes by inserting attacks

[3] This is in general the position taken by Bultmann in his great commentary on John.—R. Bultmann, *Das Evangelium des Johannes*, p. 4.

on the Baptists and the Jews. But it was not rewritten carefully enough to take away every non-Johannine phrase; thus Grace, Fullness and Logos remained. If this reconstruction is sound, we see the pre-Johannine author of the hymn making a minor use of the Stoic Logos concept. John's use of the term was, therefore, doubly minor.

It is plain that one of the least important titles for Jesus in the Fourth Gospel is that of the Logos. It is only one of many titles applied to him by the evangelist; it is applied to him only in the prologue; nowhere in the Gospel is there a discourse on Jesus the Logos—such as occur on Light, Life and Truth. The term "Logos," moreover, does not have content or associations that fit naturally into the function of the Johannine Jesus. To refer to the Jesus of this Gospel as the "Logos-Christ" is to misrepresent the message that the evangelist wrote. It would be equally reasonable to call him the "Rabbi-Christ," for he is called Rabbi on at least seven occasions (1:38, 49; 3:2; 4:31; 6:25; 9:2; 11:8). But no one would claim that Jesus actually functions here as a rabbi—a rabbi without Torah can hardly be imagined. The one instance in which Jesus interprets Scripture (10:34-36) in debate with the Jews is an example of the *argumentum ad hominem,* and sets off in sharp contrast his general practice of appealing to his own words and deeds as the supreme authority. It is not Moses who has the divine words, but

(145)

Jesus. This is said plainly in the prologue, in the sixth chapter and elsewhere. Functionally, the Jesus of John is a thousand miles removed from the Jewish rabbi.[4]

No less strange to the Jesus of this Gospel is the Logos mantle. In Stoic thinking the Logos was the divine reason that permeated the universe so that every man was born with one spark or fragment of it within him. He became the Wise Man as a result of fanning that spark into a blaze. Epictetus says, "From within come both help and destruction" (iv.9.16). Where Epictetus says "from within [*esōthen*]," John says "from above [*anōthen*]." For in John salvation comes from outside the individual—an idea that would be anathema to every Stoic. In John, no one has the Logos unless he accepts Jesus. In Stoicism, the individual develops virtues, fights vices and slowly "toils up the steep hill of virtue." In John, he believes and has eternal life now. There is no virtue except belief in Jesus and love of the brothers, no sin except to refuse to believe in him.

Johannine parallels to Stoicism are parallels in terminology alone. "Every one that sins is the slave of sin" is said both by John and by Epictetus. But in John, the sin is defined as

---

[4] If the religion of the Fourth Gospel is to have any close functional association with Judaism, it must be with some such Jewish mystery cult as Professor E. R. Goodenough has described in his book, *By Light, Light* (New Haven, 1935). But this valuable exposition of Philo is hardly sufficient evidence of the existence of a cult. See the review of S. J. Case in *The Journal of Religion*, XV (1935), 484-85.

not believing in Jesus, and the natural means of obtaining freedom from sin is to believe in Jesus. But Epictetus says to his hearers: "Emancipate yourselves! Learn to control your inclinations and aversions, restrict them to things that are within your own power—and you will be free." In significant and functional parallels Stoicism is closer to Judaism and the Synoptic Jesus than it is to John.

It may be noted by way of parenthesis that the impassivity and *apatheia* of Jesus in John would suit Stoics much better than would the compassion of Jesus in the earlier gospels. But since this would also please all Greeks of any degree of culture whatever, the specific reference to Stoicism cannot be pressed.

Our conclusion is that the use of the word "Logos" in the Johannine prologue does not indicate any direct or strong influence of Stoicism. The nearest parallel lies in Plutarch's use of the word "Logos" as a title for Osiris. Although he uses it more than once, commentators on *Isis and Osiris* do not constantly refer to Osiris as the "Logos-Osiris." For Plutarch—as for John—"Logos" is a title of minor importance; it is little more than window dressing. Plutarch much prefers other titles for Osiris, and Osiris as he interprets him functions in thoroughly non-Stoic fashion. In all these respects, Plutarch's use of Logos parallels Johannine usage.

The relation of John to contemporary philosophy in general is no more direct than its relation to Stoicism. In fact, John reveals no mastery of any intellectual discipline; he does not write for those in the Greco-Roman world who had gone through the formal disciplines of an education. No matter how loosely the word "intellectual" is defined, it will hardly include the readers of this Gospel. There is here no definition of terms, no interest in abstractions, no attempt at systematization, no knowledge or use of Greco-Roman literature or the teaching of any philosopher, no attempt to meet the standards of "Attic" composition. In these respects John is definitely below all contemporary philosophers. The Stoics were the most "popular" and the most pragmatic of philosophers. Yet when we turn from John to as humble a Stoic as Epictetus, the Phrygian slave, we cannot escape the feeling that we have entered a more rarefied intellectual atmosphere. Epictetus is interested in the definition of technical terms; he attempts to order his thoughts in a system, and he at least knows and employs the vocabulary of Stoicism. Quotations from his own teacher, Musonius Rufus, from Zeno, from Chrysippus and from Socrates appear in his sermons. He knows enough of Epicureanism to attack some of its catchwords. But John gives no indication of having mastered any philosophy even to the extent that Epictetus had mastered Stoicism.

John stands at an intellectual level a little lower than the second-century apologists, who themselves were far below contemporary philosophers—Justin's protestations to the contrary notwithstanding. These defenders of the faith had not been trained in philosophy and were not concerned with the use of philosophic techniques; they were believers in a revelation who used every conceivable argument to defend the cult and make it attractive to the pagan world. Many of their arguments came from the older Jewish apologetic movement; nor do they hesitate to indict paganism for the crimes of which they are themselves accused by pagan critics. The use of the title "Philosopher" by Aristides and Justin is intended to impress the audience. Josephus had claimed that he had studied in all the various "schools" of Jewish wisdom, which corresponded to the Greek philosophies; Justin in almost identical vein claims to have studied all varieties of pagan philosophy. In both cases this is an apologetic tool, not autobiography. Only one of the pre-Catholic apologists has any knowledge of Greco-Roman literature worth mentioning; it is not till we approach the third century that we find the Christian defenders acquainted with the contemporary culture. Geffcken's work on the apologists has demonstrated this in general and in detail.[5]

That John had less interest in things intellectual than had

[5] See, e.g., *Zwei griechische Apologeten* (Leipzig and Berlin, 1907), pp. 31-32, 250-51; and O. Staehlin, *Die altchristliche griechische Literatur* (Munich, 1924), p. 1277.

the apologists is indicated by the fact that in spite of his many agreements with their positions he did not write an apology. His work is an evangel, a gospel, not an apology or a philosophical discourse. The form in which he puts his message before his audience indicates that they were a group primarily interested in gaining *divine* aid. It is a group awaiting supernatural assistance from outside itself that first reads the Fourth Gospel. They were anxious to find salvation, to obtain eternal life. They sought some mediator, some revealer of God to bridge the gulf between man and God and give them an abiding Counselor. In short, they were salvationists and not philosophers. And the author of the Gospel hoped to convert some of them to the Christian faith, to make his written gospel the means of bringing them salvation.

One cannot speak of salvation in the Greco-Roman world without bringing to mind the mystery religions, but the first readers of the Fourth Gospel were not among those who hurried to be initiated in the cults of Isis, Mithras, Dionysus or Demeter. The parallels between Johannine Christianity and such cults as these are numerous and significant, and have been pointed out too often to need emphasis here. They are all salvation cults; their primary function is that of mediating *palingenesia* or rebirth into immortality; and a dying and rising god is the Lord of the cult. John and the mysteries agree in the nature of their theology-mythology, and in the benefits conferred upon believers.

But there is one striking functional difference. The mystery cults are sacramental in the sense that the divine benefits are obtained by going through a certain ritual—the mystery initiation. Perhaps the most striking and best-known example of a rite that carried divine blessings is the *taurobolium,* or baptism in the blood of a bull, which was very popular in the Mithras cult. The one so baptized was reborn for eternity. But the same result was achieved by practically all the mystery initiations. Professor Willoughby mentions among fundamental characteristics common to all the mysteries that they were sacramental religions, guaranteeing salvation only to those who had taken part in the necessary ceremonies. The way in which this was done in the various cults is described in his book on pagan regeneration.[6] In each of them salvation is intimately associated with the rite.

Pauline Christianity was also a sacramental religion in this sense. This is not to say that the Pauline teaching on baptism and the Lord's Supper exactly parallels the function of baptism and the sacred meal in any mystery cult. But the Pauline interpretation of the rites parallels the function of the mystery initiation as a whole, whether that initiation included any baptism and sacred meal or not. In Paul's

[6] H. R. Willoughby, *Pagan Regeneration* (Chicago, 1929).

letters those who have been baptized into the divine Lord have put on the divine Lord. The believers died with the Lord and were buried with him in baptism, in which also they were raised from the dead with him.[7] Substitute "mystery" or "initiation" for "baptism," and the Isiac or Mithraic initiate would recognize this as the teaching of his own cult. The importance of these sacraments for Paul is shown by the strenuous efforts he makes to find prototypes of both for his beloved Israel. Israel was baptized in the Red Sea; Israel ate the spiritual meal in the wilderness in the manna and the water from the rock, for Christ was the rock. Further indications of the importance of these two rites in Pauline Christianity can be seen in Paul's warnings about abuse of the Lord's Supper, in the basis of his arguments about idolatry, and in his reference to baptism for the dead.[8] But the first readers of John's Gospel were not sacramentarians of the Pauline type.

John is writing the story of Jesus, not a symbol of mystery initiation or even letters as discursive as Paul's. Could one expect more favorable treatment of baptism and the supper in a gospel? The answer is given in Mark, Matthew and Luke-Acts. They play up the baptism of Jesus as an impor-

---

[7] Gal. 3:27; Col. 2:11-12; Rom. 6:1-11. For a fuller discussion of the relation of the Pauline sacraments to the mystery initiation, see S. J. Case, *The Evolution of Early Christianity* (Chicago, 1914), chap. 10.

[8] 1 Cor. 10:1 f., 14-22; 11:17-34; 15:29.

tant act; in John it vanishes. They make much of the Last Supper; there is none in John. The solemn importance of baptism and the cup colors Mark's account of Jesus' reply to the sons of Zebedee. Baptism plays an important part in the Great Commission of Matthew 28:18 ff. and its echo in Mark 16:16. Luke needs no such emphasis at the close of his Gospel, for in his second volume his narratives plainly indicate baptism as one of the important functions of the expanding church. John, however, combines the Pentecost of Luke-Acts with the Matthaean commission (John 20:21-23), but he says not a word of baptism. Thus when every allowance has been made for John as a Gospel, it is still clear that the author finds no central place for any ritual, not even for the rites of baptism and the supper. His God is spirit, and expects a spiritual, not a ritual, worship.[9]

In this subordination of ritual to inner spiritual worship, the Johannine Gospel is similar to the Hermetic literature. In the Hermetic cult, as in John, rebirth was necessary for salvation and the teaching on rebirth is presented in a dialogue. "This dialogue took the place in a general way of the initiatory rites of the mysteries."[10] A symbolic vocabulary, emotionally powerful, is met with in this literature as in John: light and darkness, spirit, truth, knowledge of God,

[9] For a more extensive treatment of sacramentalism in John see pp. 53-56.
[10] Willoughby, *op. cit.,* p. 212.

etc. The initiates became sons of god, or entered into god. But Hermes, like the Jesus of the Fourth Gospel, is primarily a revealer rather than a savior. Or, it is perhaps more accurate to say, he saved *by revelation.* Professor Willoughby locates Hermeticism somewhere between cult and philosophy;[11] and it was for a group living in that area that John wrote the Fourth Gospel.

Hermeticism was from one viewpoint an aspect of Gnosticism.[12] The one striking difference between John and Hermeticism is, therefore, also the main difference between John and Gnosticism. The Johannine message lacks altogether the ascetic note so frequently and so strongly sounded in Gnostic writings. The candidate for the Hermetic initiation went through an ascetic preparation, for he had to learn to hate the world of sense before he could gain spiritual birth. The belief in the wickedness of matter and the consequent definition of salvation as escape from the evil world of matter has left little trace in John. Only twice does he set spirit against flesh, and each time—as we have seen—he is contrasting the spiritual meaning of a saying with its actual physical performance. He substitutes the antithesis of Christian versus non-Christian for the Gnostic antithesis of matter

[11] *Ibid.,* p. 223.

[12] While "Gnosticism" is now generally admitted to lack exact definition, it is still a useful term in that its very indefiniteness makes it possible to employ it as a blanket covering many related religious movements of the early Christian period.

and spirit. The only other Johannine dualism is that of divine versus human, of the upper world of light contrasted with the present world of darkness. But in John one does not feel, as in Orphism, Paulinism and Gnosticism, that the believer is inherently—even if partially—part of the lower world. The Johannine believer is not a dualistic microcosm, a being in which the struggle of good and evil worlds is carried on in miniature. The struggle between good and evil, light and darkness, upper and lower takes place outside the believer; it is an external process in which Jesus triumphed. The believer enters into the triumph by believing in Jesus who brought life from the divine upper world to this human world. But this much dualism colors almost every form of religious thinking in the Greco-Roman world; it was not the creation nor the exclusive possession of Gnosticism.

Paul is closer to the Gnostics here than is John, for the apostle to the Gentiles clearly regarded the flesh and sin as closely associated; such contrasts as "natural" versus "spiritual" are at home in Paul, but would sound rather strange in John. In our opinion, there can be no doubt but that John had reacted violently against some specific manifestation of Gnosticism that stressed this dualism. The proof lies not in his stressing the physical body of Jesus—for that is not emphasized—but in the care with which he avoids the word "gnosis." This catchword of the Gnostic sects does not appear even once in the Fourth Gospel, although the verbal forms occur one hundred thirty-three times. John shuns it as he would the plague because it has been appropriated by a rival (i.e., an erroneous, vicious) cult. His failure to use this word "knowledge" is paralleled by the absence of the noun "faith." Although the verb "believe" occurs ninety-five times in John, "faith" is not used a single time. This is the more striking when it is noted that this word occurs in every other book in the New Testament. It may be that "faith" like "knowledge" had already been appropriated by the Gnostics (cf. the later *Pistis Sophia*).

The extent of the Gnostic flavor in Johannine circles can be recognized by one's noting the "Johannine" elements in a summary of Bousset's description of Gnosticism.[13] Gnosticism, he says, is not an intellectual tendency chiefly concerned with philosophical speculation, but rather a religious movement. Its gnosis does not mean knowledge but revelation. It resembles the mysteries in that (a) the ultimate object is individual salvation, the assurance of a fortunate destiny for the soul after death; (b) the central object of worship is a redeemer-deity; (c) holy rites and formulas play a prominent part. Gnosticism was based on a decided oriental dualism which combined the opposition between spirit and matter with the antagonism of two hostile worlds,

[13] In his article "Gnosticism" in the *Encyclopedia Britannica*, 11th ed.

standing in contrast to each other like light and darkness. Gnosticism presented salvation as an elaborate myth which accounted for the origin of the evil world, the revelation of the *gnosis*, and the path by which man would climb out of this world.

In John the story of Jesus replaces the salvation myth. There is no asceticism. There is an emphasis on unity. There is less "speculation," either cosmological or soteriological, than is usually found in Gnostic sources. There is a disparagement of ritual rather than an emphasis on sacraments; it may have been a Gnostic sacramentarianism against which John reacted in this way. But it cannot be said too strongly that the gospel of Light, Life and Truth when it is most Johannine is very Gnostic. The objective evidence of this lies in the popularity of John's Gospel with the Gnostics of the second century. A Gnostic wrote the first commentary on the Fourth Gospel, and Loewenich, in a thorough study of the use of John down to A.D. 200, has shown that John won a rapid and widespread success among the Gnostics. They used it so extensively that he claims that it was saved for orthodoxy only by the vigorous arguments of Irenaeus.

The close resemblance in vocabulary and type of religious thinking between the Fourth Gospel and such so-called "Gnostic" writings as the Hermetic and Mandaean literature has been most ably presented by Walter Bauer in his valuable commentary on the Gospel of John. In the preface to his work, he outlines the relationship of the Fourth Gospel to the religious syncretism of the world in which it was written, and especially to that portion of it which is usually called Gnostic. He points out that the ideas of the Mandaean cult, its concepts, expressions and figures of speech, constantly remind us of John. Yet he does not regard the relation as close enough to justify an affirmation of direct dependence. This literature, in his opinion, is rather to be regarded as a rich treasury of illuminating parallels to Johannine religion and Johannine language. These parallels he has cited throughout his commentary together with all that can be drawn from other Gnostic sources. A careful reading of this material indicates that the Johannine church was largely influenced by ideas which we call Gnostic.

Rudolph Bultmann also has recognized the importance of Gnosticism for the understanding of the Fourth Gospel. In his commentary in the Meyer series, he explains the resemblances and the equally striking differences by assuming that the author used as a source a collection of sayings which contained the prologue and the great "I-am" pronouncements. This source originated in an early Gnostic group, and the evangelist transformed its Gnostic terminology into a Christian theology.

John rendered invaluable service to two different Christian

groups. One of these groups was the small local church to which he belonged; the other was the Christian church of the entire Greco-Roman world as it existed in the second century. John's service to the more inclusive group has long been recognized. The movement of Christianity from Judaism to the Gentiles created a need for a gospel more Gentile and less Jewish. John's achievement was that he retold the gospel story in a fashion that made it less Jewish in vocabulary, in religious ideology and in the type of religious experience portrayed. The expansion of the Christian church among the Gentiles was aided immeasurably by this new Gospel. Our New Testament handbooks have given John deserved acclaim for translating the gospel into a Gentile idiom.

The smaller group that John served was a Gentile group with some degree of prestige. The members of the group were not typical Christians of the second century. In the possession of a little money and a little culture, and in the extent of their interest in gnosis, they stood apart from the main stream of Christian development that led to the formation of the Catholic church. They were more anti-Semitic than the majority of the Christians;[14] they were less interested in the human Jesus; they were more concerned with a

[14] The extent to which John stands apart from the main current is suggested by his use of the Old Testament. See E. C. Colwell, "The Fourth Gospel and Early Christian Art," *The Journal of Religion* XV (1935), pp. 191-206.

contemplative mysticism and less interested in ritual than was the case with the majority of the followers of Jesus in the second century.

John's "completest" service—if the phrase be allowed—was the service rendered this minority group. This Gospel ministered to their needs in a thoroughly satisfactory fashion. They were the audience John had in mind as he wrote, and they must have perused the book with a feeling of "at-home-ness" such as no later readers have felt. Here they found a Jesus above slander and cavil; here was Truth-Light-Life gloriously mediated for them. Yet this "completest" service was at the same time the most transitory and briefest.

In the Johannine Gospel Jesus is not one among several revelations of God; he is *the* Revelation. This is indicated negatively in two ways: John is not the revelation, and the revelation is not in Judaism. It is to be observed that these two rejected media of revelation correspond to the two objects of polemical attack in our Gospel. They are attacked as false revelations precisely because they had advanced revelatory claims and Christianity could not ignore such strong competitors. The claims of Judaism were based on centuries of experience enshrined in sacred scriptures. The supporters of the Baptist as God's revelation had a serious difficulty to overcome inasmuch as novelty in religion was viewed with skepticism by antiquity. Nevertheless, the vigor of the fourth evangelist's attack indicates the considerable degree of success the followers of John had achieved in advancing their claims. And it must be remembered that Christianity itself was at this time a new religion facing the same obstacles as those confronting the movement of the Baptist.

The possibility that John the Baptist was the revelation of God is suggested by several passages. The first is in the prologue, obviously a part of the author's editorial work:

There was a man sent from God, whose name was John. He came for testimony, to bear witness to the light, that all might believe through him. *He was not the light,* but came to bear witness to the light. [1:6-8][15]

This possibility that John was the revelation is explicitly negated by this statement. It is a part of the general attempt to minimize the importance of John in the Gospel; John is not the Light, but Jesus is.

A second passage continues the analogy of light:

You sent to John, and he has borne witness to the truth. Not that the testimony which I receive is from man; but I say this that you may be saved. He was a burning and a shining lamp, and you were willing to rejoice for a while in his light. But the testimony which I have is greater than that of John. [5:33-36]

John was *a* light, but he was not *the* light. His light shone momentarily only to yield to the true light. Jesus is the sole

---

[15] Quotations in the remaining pages of this chapter are from the Revised Standard Version. Italics ours.

revelation; John but bears witness to the fact. What seemed to some to be the revelation was but an attestation of the true revelation.

The revelation is not in Judaism. Moses is not the revelation. The importance of Moses in Jewish thought is paramount. But the supremacy of Moses in symbolizing the revelation through Judaism places him for the Gospel writer in the same camp with John the Baptist. All competitors of Jesus as the revelation are dispatched with haste. Moses himself was merely a witness to Jesus: "If you believed Moses, you would believe me, for he wrote of me. But if you do not believe his writings, how will you believe my words?" (5:46-47).

But that Moses was a strong competitor as the revelation is indicated by the vigorous attack which Jesus makes on the Jews. The manna which their fathers ate was not true bread. They ate the manna and died. Jesus is the true bread which will give those who eat it eternal life. Moses himself is minimized. Moses did not give them bread from heaven; the Father gives them the true bread from heaven (6:32). Moses did not give them circumcision; it was given by the fathers (7:22). The same motif that operated in the case of John the Baptist is in force here—there is only one revelation. Not even the great Moses enshrined in centuries of sacred tradition can compete with Jesus.

Abraham is dealt with in the same manner. If the Jews were children of Abraham they would not seek to put Jesus to death. Not that Abraham is an equal of Jesus—that could never be! "Abraham died, as did the prophets," but he who keeps Jesus' word will never taste death (8:52). Abraham himself rejoiced to see "the day" of Jesus. Jesus surpassed Abraham in age. To outward appearances less than half a century old, Jesus in fact preceded Abraham in time: "Before Abraham was, I am" (8:58).

Judaism, then, is not the revelation. Moses, the custodian of the divine revelation in Torah, himself must yield to a superior revelation, and Abraham to whom the promises were given is but an infant compared with the one who pre-existed with God the Father.

That Jesus is the revelation is indicated by the references to judgment throughout the Gospel; judgment is the necessary concomitant of the revelation. In the Synoptics, judgment takes place at the end of the age, but in the Fourth Gospel judgment is present, and since judgment is present and vital the reward is present; he who believes in Jesus receives life now. This is a dominant teaching of the Gospel. Nowhere can it be seen more clearly than in the eleventh chapter:

Jesus said to her, "Your brother will rise again." Martha said to him, "I know that he will rise again in the resurrection at the last day." Jesus said to her, "I am the resurrection and the life; he who believes in me, though he die, yet shall he live, and whoever lives and believes in me shall never die." [11:23-26]

The great sin of the Jews is that God's revelation is present among them and they reject it. This is their judgment.

It might appear from certain passages that John also contains the older eschatological concept of judgment. As a result the Gospel writer has been accused of inconsistency. This problem is related to his use of the term "Son of man." At first glance it seems entirely out of place in the Fourth Gospel which has "Son of God" as its characteristic title for Jesus. The charge of inconsistency needs examination.

The passages which contain the term "Son of man" fall into several classes. The first speaks of the Son of man as descending from and returning to the Father:

"No one has ascended into heaven but he who descended from heaven, the Son of man. [3:13]
Then what if you were to see the Son of man ascending where he was before. [6:62]

The term "Son of man" is also used in passages dealing with the crucifixion of Jesus. This is not different from the preceding classification, for the "lifting up" on the cross is glorification; the cross is a ladder reaching to heaven. The passages are as follows:

As Moses lifted up the serpent in the wilderness, so must the Son of man be lifted up, that whoever believes in him may have eternal life. [3:14-15]

When you have lifted up the Son of man, then you will know that I am he, and that I do nothing on my own authority, but speak thus as the Father taught me. [8:28]

The hour has come for the Son of man to be glorified. [12:23]

"Now is the judgment of this world, now shall the ruler of this world be cast out; and I, when I am lifted up from the earth, will draw all men to myself." He said this to show by what death he was to die. The crowd answered him, "We have heard from the law that the Christ remains forever. How can you say that the Son of man must be lifted up? Who is this Son of man?" [12:31-34]

An additional passage may be placed in association with these, though its specific implication is less certain.

I say to you [Nathanael], you will see heaven opened, and the angels of God ascending and descending upon the Son of man. [1:51]

This seems to be a reference to the cross as the ladder between earth and heaven. If so, the imagery is that of Genesis 28, the vision of Jacob.

A third group of passages emphasizes the authoritative and judgmental aspect of the function of the Son of man:

Truly, truly, I say to you, the hour is coming, and now is, when the dead will hear the voice of the Son of God, and those who hear will live. For as the Father has life in himself, so has he granted the Son also to have life in himself, and has given him authority to execute judgment, because he is the Son of man. [5:25-27]

The entire passage, 12:27-50, part of which is quoted above, belongs in this category as well. In addition to the idea of judgment it contains the reference to "the last day":

He who rejects me and does not receive my sayings, has a judge; the word that I have spoken will be his judge on the last day. [12:48]

One passage speaks of eating the flesh of the Son of man and drinking his blood:

Truly, truly, I say to you, unless you eat the flesh of the Son of man and drink his blood, you have no life in you. [6:53]

This has a distinctly physical reference, as do the passages which speak of "lifting up" the Son of man. Jesus, though a divine being, was capable of being handled by men, though the examples of physical contact are exceedingly rare in this Gospel.

An analysis of these passages is very revealing. The following points may be noted:

1. The term "Son of man" is used by the Gospel writer to indicate the exalted, glorified being who came from heaven to earth, and returned in glory to the Father. Thus the idea of an exalted being, a characteristic of the Synoptic Son of

man, is retained. However, there is a difference at this point, for the older idea placed the coming of the Son of man at the end of the age while in the Fourth Gospel he has already descended from heaven with the coming of the Spirit. It would appear, then, that the Son of man and the Spirit are identified as the same by the Gospel writer. But the Son of man title preserves for him the idea of exaltation. The passages which deal with the descent from heaven, and those which relate to crucifixion are alike in their emphasis upon Jesus' exalted status.

2. In the Fourth Gospel, no less than in the Synoptics, Jesus as Son of man has a judgmental function. He has authority to exercise judgment "because he is the Son of man." It is true that the function of judgment is also denied, but that is because the author rejects the older concept of the judgmental function of the Son of man and instead emphasizes an automatic judgment: the response, positive or negative, to the revelation of God in Jesus. This is Johannine judgment. But it is well to observe that when he discusses the problem of judgment he usually speaks of Jesus as the Son of man. Thus he uses the older terminology but in the new context of a present judgment. Jesus does not need to pronounce judgment, for judgment is inherent in the fact that light has come into the world and men loved darkness rather than light.

3. The phrase "the last day" involved in the Son of man passage, on the face of it so contradictory, is in fact completely at home in this Gospel.[16] The last day, it is true, is not the day of judgment at the end of the age; it is, rather, the time of crucifixion with its attendant circumstances of glorification and the giving of the Spirit. This is indicated by two considerations.

In the first place, the "dead who are in the tombs" are not those who are physically dead any more than Lazarus who was in the tomb four days is to be thought of as a symbol of those physically dead. The writers' concern is not with flesh but with spirit. The fact that the reference to the dead coming forth from the tombs is future ought not to be pressed too far, for from the vantage point of the life of Jesus it is future—future in the same sense that the giving of the Spirit is future.

In the second place, when assessing the problem of Johannine judgment, the function of the cross should not be overlooked. The important passage is 12:27-36. Its importance is indicated by its place in the narrative. It follows the coming of the Greeks and Jesus' announcement that the time of his death (glorification) has arrived. It contains the one event in the Gospel where God speaks audibly to Jesus,

---

[16] John 12:48; cf. 6:39, 40, 44, 54; 11:24. The fact that Jesus corrects Martha (11:24-25) shows that the evangelist has adapted the phrase to his own viewpoint.

(168)

a rather amazing fact! Following the announcement of the Father that he has glorified his name and will glorify it again, Jesus says, "*Now* is the judgment of this world, *now* shall the ruler of this world be cast out; and I, when I am lifted up from the earth, will draw all men to myself" (vv. 31-32). Judgment is still in typically Johannine terms; it is related to crucifixion and the giving of the Spirit. It is this great terminus of the Gospel which is interpreted as "the last day," a terminus which itself becomes for the church a point of new beginnings. It means judgment upon the world of darkness but new life for believers. This "last day" coincides with the great day when in every Jewish home the Paschal lamb was slain.

One other aspect of the problem needs explanation. In 12:48 Jesus says: "He who rejects me and does not receive my sayings has a judge; the word that I have spoken will be his judge on the last day." If what we have said about the crucifixion as the "last day" is true then there ought to be some connection between it and the "words" of Jesus. Is this the case?

For one thing, one gains the impression on reading the account of the trial, that the Jews are the ones really being tried, not Jesus.[17] (The real issue is between Jesus and the

---

[17] The judgmental function of Jesus is emphasized dramatically if 19:13 is translated to read that *Jesus* sat on the judgment seat. Both Moffatt and Goodspeed convey this meaning. See above p. 65.

Jews, not Jesus and Pilate, for Pilate is essentially innocent.) This is judgment on the Jews and what Jesus *is* condemns them. But it should be observed that his *words* (what he has taught) are also brought into the account:

> The high priest then questioned Jesus about his disciples and his teaching. Jesus answered him, "I have spoken openly to the world; I have always taught in synagogues and in the temple, where all Jews come together; I have said nothing secretly. Why do you ask me? Ask those who have heard me, what I said to them; they know what I said." When he had said this, one of the officers standing by struck Jesus with his hand saying, "Is that how you answer the high priest?" Jesus answered him, *"If I have spoken wrongly, bear witness to the wrong; but if I have spoken rightly, why do you strike me?"*[18]

This is another example of Johannine cross reference. What Jesus *said* as well as what he *is* testifies of him.

4. There are Son of man passages which seem to suggest the physical aspect of Jesus' nature. Jesus can be lifted up from the earth as Son of man. An intermediate reference to the eating of the flesh and drinking of the blood of the Son of man has the same emphasis. Would the writer have used the term "Son of God" in the same connections or is his choice of terms deliberate? It is a bare possibility that here we find indications of the older connotation "man" attaching to his use of the title. This is doubtful, however, owing

[18] 18:19-23.

to the fact that the Son of man comes down from heaven and returns to the Father. If the generic meaning of the term remains at all, it is merely as a means of suggesting in strategic instances the vestiges of the human which remained with Jesus. It is our opinion that this cannot be pressed very far.

The conclusion reached from this study of Johannine judgment is that in no case does it depart from the central theme that judgment is present and automatic. Jesus is not a judge in the eschatological sense; he never *pronounces* judgment. Judgment is inherent in the response made to Jesus. The burden of choice is, therefore, on the individual himself. The cross is crucial to the problem of judgment for it separates the enemies of Jesus from the believers. The Jews are destined to die but the believers are to be recipients of the Spirit which gives eternal life. The cross is, for the Gospel writer, the great line of demarcation; it is the Johannine judgment seat! But it is so only because he who was crucified was the sole revelation of God. The revelation sets before men life or death; theirs is the choice. The Jews chose death, the believers life.

That Jesus is the sole revelation of God is set forth under a series of names applied to him. He is Life, Light, Truth, the Shepherd, the Door, the Way, the Vine.[19]

[19] For a discussion of the title "Lamb of God" see p. 16.

Jesus is Life! This note is first struck in the prologue: "In him was life" (1:4); but the idea runs throughout the Gospel. In the story of the Samaritan woman, Jesus gives "living" water, i.e., water that gives life. But the analogy of water is directly joined with the concept of the Spirit. When the individual believes on Jesus, "out of his heart shall flow rivers of living water" (7:38), and, the evangelist adds, Jesus said this about the Spirit which was yet to be given. Thus, Jesus as life-giver is Jesus as spirit.

Just as Jesus is living water, so also he is living bread. Again, it is the bread which gives life. He is contrasted with the manna in the wilderness; this is inferior bread. The fathers ate of it and died. Jesus, on the other hand, is the true bread from heaven which bestows eternal life upon him who partakes.

This idea of eternal life is a dominant note of the Fourth Gospel. This is the Johannine counterpart of the Synoptic Kingdom of God. The quality of God's love for the world is indicated by the fact that he gave his only Son so that men might have eternal life instead of death (3:16). The nearest approach to a definition of eternal life comes in 17:3: "This is eternal life that they might know thee the only true God, and Jesus Christ whom thou hast sent." But one does not start with a knowledge of God and come to believe in Jesus. Knowledge of God in this Gospel comes through Jesus:

"No one has ever seen God; the only Son, who is in the bosom of the Father, he has made him known" (1:18). The closest approximation to an understanding of Jesus from a knowledge of God is in 7:16-17:

> So Jesus answered them [the Jews], "My teaching is not mine, but his who sent me; if any man's will is to do his will, he shall know whether the teaching is from God or whether I am speaking on my own authority."

But this is purely hypothetical since the Jews of the Fourth Gospel are not children of God, so have no way to check the truth of Jesus' words on this basis (8:47). Knowledge of God comes through him and him alone and gives eternal life.

Life eternal, then, comes through *gnosis,* knowledge. It is not intellectual knowledge but supernatural revelation. And this revelation in the Fourth Gospel does not impinge upon the consciousness apart from the revelation in Jesus— he *is* the revelation. Man's part is to believe; the result is the gift of eternal life. Thus eternal life is closely related to the fact of Jesus himself. As E. F. Scott pointed out, life is something embodied in the Person of Christ:

> Into this world of darkness and death He came as the living One, and in order to receive His gift we require to participate in His being and nature. The whole teaching of the Gospel is determined by this thought, that the life is bound up with the

Person, and that the work of Christ consists in the last resort in the communication of Himself.[20]

The Revelation of God carries in himself the life of God. This is the content of the revelation.

To understand the nature of eternal life it is necessary to keep in mind that for the fourth evangelist Jesus is God. The life which resides in him is essential, elemental life. It is not subject to death any more than God is subject to death. Through belief the individual appropriates this life for himself. On this account he too becomes victorious over death. Eternal life is therefore endless, but endlessness is not its primary characteristic. The emphasis must be placed on its quality. The believer comes to share in the life of his god and gains for himself the same benefits.

But to all who received him, who believed in his name, he gave power to become children of God; who were born, not of blood nor of the will of the flesh nor of the will of man, but of God. [1:12-13]

Belief in Jesus makes possible this birth from above, this change of nature, this sharing in the nature of Christ and God.

A second figure under which John depicts Jesus as the revelation is that of light. We have already seen the relation

[20] E. F. Scott, *The Fourth Gospel: Its Purpose and Theology*, p. 283.

of the word "light" to Gnosticism;[21] also its usage in relation to the lesser light, John the Baptist.[22] It remains to point out two additional features associated with the word.

For one thing, Matthew had recorded Jesus as saying to the disciples, "You are the light of the world" (Matt. 5:14). But this could never be for John; there is only one Light of the World and that is Jesus. Therefore he has Jesus say, "I am the light of the world" (8:12). And again, "As long as I am in the world, I am the light of the world." Jesus, then, is the light-giver. That is certainly the inner meaning of the healing of the blind man (9:1-41).

Second, the concept of judgment is related to the figure of Jesus as Light. The spiritual significance of the healing of the blind man is set forth in 9:39-41. The Jews are the ones who "see," i.e., claim sight, but demonstrate their blindness by failure to recognize Jesus as God's revelation; therefore their sin remains. The light judges them and they are condemned.

The same association of light with judgment is made in 12:27-36. Jesus is the Light; he is to be with them for a "little longer." Soon the Light will be withdrawn and darkness will come upon the world. While they have the Light they must believe in the Light that they may be Sons of Light.

[21] See p. 157.
[22] See p. 161.

(vv. 35-36). All of this is presented to the crowd, which refused to believe in accordance with Isaiah's words:

He has blinded their eyes and hardened their heart, lest they should see with their eyes and perceive with their heart, and turn for me to heal them.

Any hope for their deliverance is dependent upon their response to Jesus, but they are incapable of a positive response.

Jesus is presented also as the Truth. It is suggested in the statement, "I am the way and the truth and the life (14:6).[23] There is recurring emphasis on the true, i.e., the genuine, as contrasted with the false throughout the Gospel: Jesus is the *true* light, he is the *true* bread, he is the *true* vine. It is a way of emphasizing the genuine character of the revelation of God in Jesus as contrasted with spurious claims.

A far more important passage representing Jesus as Truth is in the account of the trial before Pilate (18:33-38). In the Synoptics, Pilate asks Jesus, "Are you the King of the Jews?" Jesus answers, "You say it." But in John his answer begins: "My kingdom is not of this world. If my kingdom were a kingdom of this world, my servants would have struggled to prevent my being handed over to the Jews. But now (you can see from their inactivity) my kingdom is not in that area" (18:36). Pilate has no need for anxiety as to Jesus'

[23] Macgregor thinks that the two substantives "truth" and "life" may serve to define the first so that the translation might read, "I am the real (true) and living way." G. H. C. Macgregor, *The Gospel of John*, p. 306.

kingly claims in John, for the realm of which Jesus is king is not temporal but eternal. He is King of Truth and so presents no threat to Rome.

The kingship of Jesus is highlighted by the title "Jesus of Nazareth, the King of the Jews" which was placed on the cross by Pilate. Written in Hebrew, Latin and Greek it suggested thereby the universal significance of Jesus. The Jews, so the story goes, wanted Pilate to change the superscription so as to read, "This man said, 'I am King of the Jews.'" Pilate refused to do so. In the end the title stood as originally written so that all men might know that he is indeed King.

Another method of indicating that Jesus is the sole revelation of God is by using the symbolism of the shepherd (10:1-18). Jesus is the Good Shepherd as distinguished from false shepherds. All who preceded Jesus were thieves and robbers (v. 8). It is doubtful if this refers to men like Abraham and Moses. To be sure, they are Jesus' inferiors but they are not his enemies. It is equally doubtful if it refers to the Pharisees to whom Jesus has been speaking. The Gospel does not seem to consider the average religious leader as a serious competitor of Jesus. It is more likely that the Gospel writer has in mind competitors of Jesus on the Messianic level. That he is thinking of *Jewish* leaders here, however, is made clear by the statement, "And I have other sheep, that are not of this fold" (v. 16).

(177)

The reference may be to false Messiahs like Judas and Theudas (Acts 5:33-39) and possibly Bar Kokhba. This, too, may be the explanation of the enigmatic passage 5:43, "I have come in my Father's name, and you do not receive me; if another comes in his own name, him you will receive."

If this is so, then the writer's argument is as follows: These so-called Messiahs are false shepherds who, because of their false character, are unable to lead the sheep. Their attempts to do so lead to disastrous consequences. Note the description of the Theudas and Judas movements of Acts 5:36-37.

For before these days Theudas arose, giving himself out to be somebody, and a number of men, about four hundred, joined him; but he was slain and all who followed him were dispersed and came to nothing. After him Judas the Galilean arose in the days of the census and drew away some of the people after him; he also perished, and all who followed him were scattered.

Jesus, on the other hand, is the Good Shepherd (the true Christ), whom the sheep will follow because they know him as their own. Instead of leading them to destruction, he gives them eternal life.

It may be objected that men like Judas and Theudas also died on behalf of their cause and therefore meet the standard set by Jesus, "The good shepherd lays down his life for the sheep" (v. 11). But this is to miss the point of the discussion.

Jesus differs from them in this respect that no one takes his life from him; he lays it down of his own accord: "I have power to lay it down, and I have power to take it again" (v. 18).

This means that Jesus moves on a level which is superior to that of his competitors. They operate on the level of political ambition and military conquest. The result is death and destruction for all concerned. Jesus, on the other hand, moves on the level of religion. His leadership results in the possession of eternal life. He alone has the qualifications of the Good Shepherd.[24]

Related to the concept of Jesus as the Good Shepherd is that of Jesus as the Door. The figure is mixed with that of the Good Shepherd. This is an example of how freely the mind of the author seized upon symbols to illustrate his idea of Jesus. There is but one way to enter into the sheepfold, and that is through Jesus, the Door. But the dominant figure throughout chapter ten is that of the shepherd.

Not only is Jesus the Door but he is the Way (14:5-6). The leading statement of verse four ("And you know the way where I am going") is deliberately introduced into the discussion. It is as though the Gospel writer had a special reason

---

[24] The figure of Jesus as the shepherd is common on the walls of the catacombs. Its literary antecedents are numerous Old Testament passages particularly, as far as John is concerned, Jer. 23:1-4; Ezek. 34:1-31. Possible New Testament sources are Mark 6:34; Acts 20:28-29.

for an exposition of the key word "way." It may be that he had in mind the early designation of Christianity as the Way (Acts 9:2; 19:9, 23; 22:4; 24:22). If this is the explanation, then our Gospel is pointing not to the Christian movement as the Way, but rather to its central figure: Christ himself is the way to the Father (14:6). The emphasis is on the Person, not on the institution.

The evangelist uses the familiar figure of the vine to suggest God's revelation in Jesus. Jesus is the True Vine (15:1-17). The use of allegory is pressed further here than anywhere else in the Gospel. Jesus is the vine, the disciples are the branches, God is the vine-dresser.

There are two leading ideas in the passage. First, since Jesus is the vine the branches must draw their life from him. Evidence of this vital relationship is fruitfulness. It is therefore the test of discipleship (v. 8). The life which the disciples draw from the True Vine expresses itself in the fulfillment of Jesus' commandment that they love one another as he has loved them (v. 12). Thus fruitfulness is defined in terms of loving relationships.

But some branches fail to meet this test. This constitutes the second element in the account. Since some branches do not bear fruit they are obviously not abiding in, i.e., not drawing their life from, the Vine. Consequently, they must be cut off and destroyed.

It is important to note that in verse three the idea of pruning is conveyed by the same word which is used in the story of Jesus washing the disciples' feet, "Jesus said to him [Peter], 'He who has bathed does not need to wash, except for his feet, but he is clean all over; and you are clean, but not all of you.' For he knew who was to betray him; that was why he said, 'You are not all clean'" (13:10-11). The word for clean is $\kappa\alpha\theta\alpha\rho\delta s$. The two passages seem to be joined by a cross reference in 15:3, "You are already made clean ($\kappa\alpha\theta\alpha\rho\omega i$) by the word which I have spoken to you." The washing of the disciples' feet is therefore a cleansing of the group, or to use the language of chapter fifteen, it is a pruning away of the false branches so that only the fruitful ones remain. This accounts for the fact that Judas at this time goes out into the night and the Beloved Disciple makes his appearance. This is the true church cleansed of its false members. The fifteenth chapter makes the same point through the use of allegory. Mere association with the group does not constitute true discipleship; what is required is a vital relationship with the Source of Life itself and that is to be found only in Jesus.

Thus the fourth evangelist sets forth the fact of God's revelation in Jesus. He approaches the problem not as a philosopher but as a religious leader concerned with the problem of salvation. For him Jesus as the Spirit makes possible Jesus as the Revelation. In this manner are brought together the two great emphases of our Gospel. Jesus is the true Revelation because the Spirit was given to him without measure.

INDEX OF NAMES AND SUBJECTS

Anothen, 44, 50, 58, 124, 126, 146
Apocryphal Gospels, 28-30
Aristides, 86 n.23, 90 n.35, 149

Bacon, B. W., Preface, 32 n.14, 108 n.1
Baptism of Jesus, 14, 107-13, 152-54
Barnabas, Epistle of, 86 n.21
Bauer, W., 87 n.27, 142 n.1, 157
Betrayal, 81-85
Bousset, 156 n.13
Bowen, Clayton R., 33 n.15
British Museum Gospel, 29 n.12
Bultmann, Rudolf, 31 n.13, 51 n.4, 67 n.10, 75 n.1, 108 n.1, 123 n.17, 144 n.3, 158
Burkitt, F. C., 25 n.5

Cabrol, F., 92 n.43, 44
Cadbury, H. J., 27 n.7, 28 n.9
Case, S. J., 32 n.14, 105 n.78, 146 n.4, 152 n.7
Celsus, 77 n.2, n.3, 78 n.5, 82 n.10, 85 n.15, n.16, 87 n.26, 89 n.31, 90 n.34, 95 n.57, n.58, 96 n.59, n.60
Christian Freedom, 17-19
Colwell, Ernest C., 99 n.66, 159 n.14
Crucifixion, 88-105

Dalton, O. M., 92 n.44, n.45
Dialogue Pattern, 56-58

Distinctive Material in John, 35 f.
Dodd, C. H., 142 n.1
Double Meanings, 44 f., 58-59
Dramatic Quality, 45, 64-66

Epictetus, 146, 148
Eschatology, 49-50, 163-71
Eusebius, 26 n.6, 36 n.18

Family of Jesus, 113-16
Feeding of Five Thousand, 54-56, 153
Friedlaender, L., 85 n.14

Galilee, 117 ff.
Geffcken, J., 149 n.5
Gethsemane, 76-81
Glory, 73 f., 122
Gnosticism, 154-58
Goguel, Maurice, 79 n.6, n.7
Goodenough, E. R., 146 n.4
Goodspeed, E. J., 8, 23 n.1, 25 n.4, 99 n.66, 125 n.19, 169 n.17
Grant, F. C., 143 n.2

Harnack, A. von, 24 n.2, n.3
Heitmueller, W., 34 n.16, n.17, 97 n.62, 102 n.71
Hermeticism, 153 f.
Historicity, 12 f.
Hosius, Carl, 91 n.38
Humility, 73-76

Ignatius, 23, 94 n.52, 95 n.53

James, M. R., 8, 29 n.10, n.11, 86 n.22, 109 n.5
Jerusalem, 117 ff.
John the Baptist, 130-35, 161
Judaism, 162 ff.
Justin Martyr, 86 n.24, 89 n.29, 95 n.54, n.55, n.56, 149

Kaufmann, C. M., 91 n.41, 92 n.45

Lamb of God, 16
Lazarus, 46 f.
Lightfoot, R. H., 32 n.14
Logos, 71, 143-47
Loewenich, W. von, 157
Luke's Purpose, 26-28
Lyman, M. E., 32 n.4

Macgregor, G. H. C., 8, 65 n.8, 67, 68, 69, 70, 112 n.8, 176 n.23
Marcion, 23
Mark's Purpose, 24 f.
Marucchi, O., 93 n.44
Matthew's Purpose, 25
Moehlman, C. H., 86 n.17
Moffatt, James, 66 n.9, 67, 169 n.17
Mystery Religions, 150 ff.

Nicodemus, 124-25

Omissions in John, 32-34

Pauline Ideas, 48-52

Philo, 91 n.37
Preisendanz, K., 99 n.66, 106 n.79

Reich, Hermann, 90 n.36, 91 n.39, n.40, 92 n.42
Resurrection, 16 f.

Sacramentalism, 50-56, 151-52
Samaritan Woman, 60-64, 127-30, 139
Schanz, Martin, 91 n.38
Scott, E. F., 8, 32 n.14, 42, 139 n.28, 142 n.1, 174 n.20
Signs, 123 f.
Son of Man, 166-71
Sources in John, 30 ff., 42-43, 142 f.
Staehlin, O., 149 n.5
Stoicism, 142 f.
Streeter, B. H., 27 n.8
Stupid Characters, 43
Symbols, 44 f., 60-64

Tacitus, 85 n.13
Taylor, Vincent, 27 n.8, 83 n.11
Tenderness, 19 f.
Tertullian, 87 n.25, 91 n.38
Tischendorf, C., 77 n.4
Transactionalism, 48-49
Transpositions, 66-70
Treatment of Sources, 36-41, 46 ff.
Trial before Pilate, 85-88
Types, 45

Willoughby, H. R., 151 n.6, 153 n.10, 154 n.11
Windisch, Hans, 37 n.19
Wrede, W., 32 n.14, 97 n.62

INDEX OF REFERENCES TO SCRIPTURE

THE OLD TESTAMENT

GENESIS

28 165

II KINGS

17:24 ff. 63

PSALMS

2:7 107
22:18 .... 102 n.70
69:21 f. 104 n.75

JEREMIAH

23:1-4 .... 179 n.24

EZEKIEL

34:1-31 .... 179 n.24

ZECHARIAH

9:9 75

THE NEW TESTAMENT

MATTHEW

2:5 .... 135 n.26
3:17 .... 110 n.7
5:14 175
8:5-13 37
8:11-21 39
17:22-23 .... 98 n.64
20:17-19 .... 98 n.64
21:1-7 102
26:38 .... 78 n.5
26:52-54 .... 94 n.50
26:69-75 72
27:24-25 .... 86 n.19
27:35 .... 102 n.69
27:39-44 .... 90 n.33

MATTHEW—*continued*

27:46-49 .... 104 n.73
27:51-53 .... 105 n.77
28:18 ff. 153

MARK

1:1 24
1:8 .... 131 n.23, 133 n.24
1:11 .... 110 n.7
1:12 124
1:14 131
2:7 .... 135 n.26
2:12 74
2:27 18
3:31-35 .... 114 n.10
4:40 74
5:15 74
5:42 74
6:34 .... 179 n.24
8:29 f. 80 n.8
8:31 .... 94 n.51, 98 n.65
9:1 .... 94 n.51
9:12 .... 98 n.65
10:32-34 .... 98 n.64
14:34 .... 78 n.5
14:66-72 72
15:24 .... 102 n.69
15:29-32 .... 90 n.33
15:32 31
15:33, 38 .... 105 n.77
15:34-36 .... 104 n.73
15:39 31
16:16 153

INDEX OF REFERENCES TO SCRIPTURE

LUKE

3:22	110 n.7
5:21	135 n.26
7:1-10	37
7:9	37, 39
9:43-45	98 n.64
14:26-27	114 n.11
16:19-31	46
18:10-13	18
18:31-34	98 n.64
22:3-6	83 n.11
22:43-44	79
22:54-62	72
22:67-71	31
23:4, 14-16, 21-22	86 n.20
23:34	102 n.69
23:35-39	90 n.33
24:45-47	94 n.49

JOHN

1:4	172
1:6-8	161
1:6-8, 15	143
1:6, 15	130
1:12-13	174
1:14, 17-18	143
1:14	59 n.7, 122
1:18	173
1:19 ff.	68
1:19-23	130
1:20	110
1:24-34	131
1:26	132
1:28	133
1:29	110
1:29-34	70, 108
1:29, 36	16
1:31	111, 131
1:32	108
1:32-33	68
1:32-34	133
1:35 f.	131
1:38, 49	145

JOHN—*continued*

1:45	101 n.68, 116 n.14
1:45-46	119
1:51	165
2:1-4	112
2:1-11	38, 68, 122
2:4	59 n.7
2:11	74
2:12, 13	69
2:13-22	56
2:17	101 n.68
2:19-21	81
2:23	38
2:23-24	58
3:1	68
3:1-21	124
3:2	145
3:3	44, 50, 58
3:3-5	33
3:5-8	59
3:13	69, 164
3:14	59, 68, 81, 97 n.61, 101
3:14-15	165
3:16	11, 16, 172
3:17, 34	120 n.15
3:21	69
3:22-30	69
3:22-31	134
3:23	133
3:24	131
3:25-30	132
3:26	132
3:31	125
3:31-36	69, 126
4:1	132
4:1 f.	134
4:1-26	127
4:1-42	60
4:4-6	128 n.21
4:7-26	57
4:10	61
4:13-14	139 n.30

INDEX OF REFERENCES TO SCRIPTURE

JOHN—*continued*

4:24	129
4:25-26	129
4:27	74
4:31	145
4:43	38
4:43-45	118
4:45	38
4:46	68
4:46-54	37
4:47	38
4:54	38
5:18	68
5:21, 25	128
5:23, 30	120 n.15
5:25-27	166
5:30-32	67
5:33	68
5:33-36	161
5:39-40, 46	101 n.68
5:41 ff.	67
5:45 ff.	67
5:46-47	162
5:47	67
6:1-65	53
6:14	74
6:25	145
6:25 ff.	54
6:26	54
6:27	126
6:29, 38, 44, 57	120 n.15
6:32	162
6:38	120
6:39-40, 44, 54	168 n.16
6:41-42	116 n.14, 119
6:45	108 n.68
6:51	55
6:62	164
6:63	55, 124, 128
6:64	82
6:71	98
7:1	67

JOHN—*continued*

7:6	59 n.7
7:14	68
7:15	68, 74
7:15-24	67
7:16-17	67, 173
7:16, 18, 28, 33	120 n.15
7:18	67
7:19	67
7:20	67
7:21	67, 68, 74
7:22	162
7:25	67
7:30	84
7:31	67
7:32	84
7:33	68
7:37-39	127, 139 n.29
7:38	172
7:38, 42	101 n.68
7:40-42	116 n.14
7:40-43	119
7:44-46	84
7:50	68
7:50-52	119
7:52	72
8:12	175
8:18, 26, 29, 42	120 n.15
8:20	84
8:28	97 n.61, 165
8:28, 50	59 n.7
8:31-51	57
8:42	120
8:47	173
8:52	163
8:52-59	58
8:58	163
9:1-41	175
9:1 ff.	68
9:2	145
9:33, 39-41	59 n.7
9:38	74

INDEX OF REFERENCES TO SCRIPTURE

JOHN—*continued*

9:39-41 175
10:1-18 177
10:7 .... 59 n.7
10:8 177
10:11 178
10:16 177
10:17-18 100
10:18 179
10:30 16
10:31 68
10:33 68
10:34-36 145
10:39 84
10:40 133
11:1 ff. 68
11:4, 11-22 .... 59 n.7
11:8 .... 68, 145
11:23-26 164
11:24 .... 122, 168 n.16
11:24-25 .... 168 n.16
11:26 16
11:37 68
11:41 122
11:45 74
11:49-50 68
12:4 98
12:4-6 .... 83 n.12
12:5 f. 33
12:9 68
12:14-16 100
12:20-22 60
12:23 165
12:24 60
12:27-30 78
12:27-36 .... 168, 175
12:27-50 166
12:28 122
12:31-32 169
12:31-34 165
12:32 f. 68, 97 n.61
12:35-36 176

JOHN—*continued*

12:37-41 101
12:44-45, 49 .... 120 n.15
12:58 ...... 166, 168 n.16, 169
13:3 .... 100 n.67
13:10-11 181
13:16 .... 33, 68
13:18 101
13:20 .... 120 n.15
13:20-36 99
13:21-28 83
13:27-30 83
13:33 68
13:34 f. 37
14:2-3 68
14:5-6 179
14:6 .... 176, 180
14:9 16
14:12 21
14:26 21
14:28 .... 16, 68
14:30-31 84
14:31 70
15:1 70
15:1-17 180
15:3 181
15:8 180
15:12 180
15:12-13 19
15:20 68
15:25 101
16:28 120
16:33 .... 70, 104 n.72
17:1 122
17:3 172
17:5 123
17:12 .... 68, 85, 101
17:13 99
17:18 68
17:22 .... 122, 123
18:2, 5 98
18:4-6 80

(188)

JOHN—*continued*

18:5, 7	120
18:8-9	85
18:9	68
18:10-11	80
18:14	68
18:17	72
18:19-23	88, 170 n.18
18:25	72
18:26	72
18:32	68, 88, 97 n.63
18:33-38	176
18:39	87
19:1-5	87
19:4, 6	87
19:5	45
19:7	68
19:7-12	87
19:9, 32	101
19:11	88
19:13	65, 169 n.17
19:19	120
19:23-24	101
19:26	104 n.74
19:26-27	115 n.13
19:28	101
19:30	104 n.76
19:31-37	101
19:39	68
20:13-17	99
20:17	99
20:19-23	134
20:21	31, 68
20:21-23	135, 153
20:22-23	123
20:29	129
20:31	32

ACTS

2:1-4	137
2:2	123
2:13	123
2:16-17	123

ACTS—*continued*

2:23	97
2:36	86 n.20
3:13-14	86 n.20
4:8	137
4:10	86 n.20
4:31	137
5:1-11	137
5:31	97
5:33-39	178
5:36-37	178
5:43	178
6:10	137
7:52	86 n.20
8:4-24	61
8:5 ff.	60
8:18	137
8:20	61
8:26-40	60
8:29	137
9:2	180
10:19-20	137
13:4	137
13:9	137
13:27-29	86 n.20
16:6	137
16:15, 31, 34	39 n.20
18:8	39 n.20
18:24	133 n.25
19:2-7	137
19:7	133 n.25
19:9, 23	180
20:22	137
20:28-29	179 n.24
21:11	137
22:4	180
23:1-5	88 n.28
24:22	180
28:25-28	137

ROMANS

6:1-11	152 n.7

INDEX OF REFERENCES TO SCRIPTURE

I CORINTHIANS

10:1 f., 14-22 .... 152 n. 8
11:17-34 .... 152 n.8
11:23 .... 81 n.9
15:3 .... 93 n.47
15:29 .... 152 n.8
15:42-50 125
15:45 .... 128, 138

II CORINTHIANS

1:21-22 127
3:17 .... 138 n.27
5:16 22
13:4 .... 89 n.32

GALATIANS

3:27 .... 152 n.7
5:11 .... 89 n.30
5:22-23 20

EPHESIANS

1:13-14 127
4:30 127

PHILIPPIANS

2:6-11 .... 93 n.48

COLOSSIANS

2:11-12 .... 152 n.7

I THESSALONIANS

2:15 .... 86 n.18